I Seen a Million Sparrows

I Seen a Million Sparrows

by

Jocelyn Reichel

Illustrated by
Martha Reichel Hekman

MOODY PRESS
CHICAGO

All Scripture quotations in this book, except those noted otherwise,
are from the *New American Standard Bible*, © 1960, 1962, 1963,
1968, 1971, 1972, 1973, 1975, and 1977 by The Lockman Foundation.

Library of Congress Cataloging in Publication Data

Reichel, Jocelyn.
    I seen a million sparrows.

    1. Reichel, Jocelyn.   2. Teachers—United States—
Biography. I. Title.
LA2317.R4A35   1983   371.1'0092'4   [B]   83-735
ISBN 0-8024-0185-6

        1 2 3 4 5 6 7 Printing/BC/Year 87 86 85 84 83

Printed in the United States of America

To Dee Everett

Contents

1
In Two Hundred
Words or Less

If you were an education major with a minor in English at Chicago Teachers College, you were probably scared to death of flunking Microbiology/Physiology, a required science class. So you planned ahead and arranged to take the summer course, a semester's work telescoped into a six-week period and taught by Dr. Goldfarb.

Professor Goldfarb was short and chubby with a cherubic, apple-cheeked countenance that belied his true nature. His wit was acerbic, his tongue a scalpel, and his victims legion. Nevertheless, he was the most popular instructor in his department. We figured it must have been his tangential tendencies; it didn't take much of a distraction to divert the good doctor from the lecture at hand to something dearer to his heart than science. Fortunately, he was a raconteur of the first order, a born ham, who took more delight in entertaining than in edifying his students. This particular course in which I was enrolled, the combination package of microbiology and physiology–calculatingly taken during a steamy Chicago summer–required a great deal of comic relief, and the professor was always happy to oblige.

"Obliging" was what he was doing on the day I have in mind. Ten minutes into the period he laid down his pointer, picked up his pipe, and began to recount some of his experiences as an assistant to the registrar. Because our college was a small one, most of the instructors had duties outside the classroom. Dr. Goldfarb's administrative stint involved the screening of applicants.

"You'd never believe—" the professor chuckled, challenging our gullibility "—the crazy reasons that people give for wanting to become teachers!"

We leaned forward, anxious to laugh along with the doctor. If rumors could be trusted, a merry heart in this class was not only physically healthy, but academically judicious. A ripple of a smile moved across the room—an anticipatory and condescending smile. Especially condescending. Ours was a class of seniors and graduate students, all within a few weeks of either commencement or certification. The professor's frequent and candid confidences about the foibles and fakeries in high places and the duncery behind the scenes—unethical though they may have been—flattered us into delusions of superiority and drew us into an esoteric circle from which we looked out upon the world with insufferable smugness.

In retrospect, I recognize the psychological process: the doctor provided the familiarity that encouraged our contempt and, in turn, nourished our famished egos. Hence, our own warm admiration for the professor. However, at that point in time, we were not concerned with analyzing his iconoclasm; we were too grateful for the diversions that delivered us from test tubes and textbooks.

Doctor Goldfarb's "you'd never believe—" had achieved its purpose—it held us in thrall while he assembled his smoking materials. I shifted my weight carefully—lab stools do not come in dowager proportions—fanned myself with a sheaf of mimeographed worksheets, and waited for the professor to finish the ministrations to his pipe.

"I remember a classic example," he resumed at last. "We all got a real charge out of this one. We still do." He began to chuckle, checked his mirth, and continued. "This applicant wrote—as all of *you* did—" he paused, leveling the pipe stem at the class "—that she wanted to become a teacher because she *loved* children!"

We laughed self-consciously, admitting the truth of his accusation.

He returned to scouring his pipe, permitting us to stew awhile in our collective guilt.

"*Imagine!*" he thundered, startling us back to attention. "*Because she loved children! Nobody* becomes a teacher because she loves kids. If there's any reason for *not* becoming a teacher, it's because you love the little monsters."

He was pacing the boards now. "Love of money? Now there's a legitimate reason. Love of prestige? Why not? Love of power? Without a doubt! But love of children? Not on your life. Anybody who loves children has no business in the classroom. Right?"

We nodded in fervent affirmation. Most of us still bore the scars from our first semester of student teaching.

"Right on, Doctor!" seconded a voice from the back of the room, a toady making sure his vote registered—clinching his "A," as it were.

There was another lengthy pause while the doctor stoked and tapped and lit and relit his pipe, fully aware of the tantalizing effect of the delay.

"Because she loved children!" he returned to the refrain with a derisive snort. "Wouldn't have been so bad if she had stopped there—with just a bald-faced lie on her record. No, she had to go ahead and amplify the falsehood—embroider and embellish it—*ad nauseam!*"

A few short, restorative puffs, and he was able to continue.

"You know where she went from there? To poetry! She quoted poetry. 'The world is so full of a number of things. . .' Have to give her credit, though," he parenthesized. "She did cite her source: Robert Louis Stevenson. 'The world is so full of a number of things,'" he went on, singsonging the lines. "'I'm sure we should all be as happy as kings!'"

There was a nervous tittering, but a scowl and an upraised eyebrow silenced it, signifying there was more to come.

11

" 'I want to take the little ones by the hand,' this future teacher wrote. 'I want to lead them along the lanes of learning, down the avenues of awareness, through the deeps of discovery...' " Dr. Goldfarb had pulled out all the stops now. Slipping into a reedy falsetto and setting aside his pipe, he minced affectedly down the aisle, clutching the hands of imaginary tykes.

" 'I want,' " he projected over the tumult, " 'to be a Pied Piper and guide youngsters out of the darkness of ignorance and into the light of knowledge. I want to place in their grubby little hands the key to happiness, which is learning—' "

He was unable to finish. The laughter—hearty, table-pounding, rolling-in-the-aisle mirth—broke out spontaneously, triggered as much by his performance as by the high-flown muddled metaphors. There wasn't a dry eye in the lab.

"Oh, that's good!" my tablemate gasped.

"That's a classic!" another student agreed, holding his aching ribs.

"Doctor," panted Mr. Right On, "you done outdid yourself!"

The professor, gratified with the response, knocked the embers from his pipe and sent us home an hour early.

Three years before the above episode, on another humid August afternoon, I had sat at my dining room table, trying to concentrate on the task before me while my four children kibitzed at my elbow. In two hundred words or less, I was supposed to tell the registrar at Chicago Teachers College why I wished to become a teacher. The rest of the application was already completed, all information duly entered and neatly typed on my husband's antique Smith-Corona. Now, pen in sweaty hand, I was attempting to write in my best Palmer script the reasons for my aspiration.

"Level with them, Mom," counseled thirteen-year-old Tom. "Tell them you never got your fill of washing blackboards when you were in school."

Well, I hadn't. That was a responsibility reserved for

Dr. Goldfarb minced affectedly down the aisle, clutching the hands of imaginary tykes.

the "best student of the day" by teachers who borrowed their psychology from Tom Sawyer. They made it a coveted privilege, and more often than not, the "best students" were actually the worst delinquents, undergoing temporary remissions for the joys of board-washing.

"That's not the *real* reason," contradicted fourteen-year-old Martha. "Just tell them that you can do as well or better than any teacher your children have ever had."

My husband, Everett, snorted ungraciously from behind his newspaper, probably recognizing Martha's contribution as a direct quote from her mother.

"I think," offered nine-year-old Debby, who seemed to have been born with a profound respect for things financial, "you ought to tell them you need the money."

"And the summer vacation," added Joanna, who at the age of five was worried about my taking a job that might leave her at the mercy of her older siblings.

I dismissed my "cabinet" and postponed my essay until later in the day. In the meantime, I reflected on the children's candid suggestions. True, I had to prepare myself for a well-paying career. Debby, who'd had arthritis since infancy, was given a bleak prognosis by the family doctor—possible complete immobility by adolescence. In and out of hospitals most of her young life, no wonder she was concerned about money!

Joanna had a point, too. Whatever work I undertook, the hours would have to coincide with those of the children. Everett and I had strong ideas about turning our youngsters over to sitters, no matter how competent. A teaching career with its excellent pay and convenient hours—not to mention the promise of being able to wash blackboards to my heart's content—seemed to be the answer. The hurdle that lay ahead, four years of college, didn't daunt me. I had reached the young, optimistic, dragon-slaying age of thirty-three.

By the time my children were in bed that night, I had decided how I would handle the answer to the query "Why do you wish to become a teacher?"

"I'm going to be altruistic," I told Everett as I spread peanut butter on his sandwiches and poured coffee into his thermos. "Altruism with a dash of the literary," I reiterated, keeping in mind that my minor would be English. My husband agreed that the combination would be irresistible and I was as good as in. He kissed me good-bye and left for his night job.

Alone at last, I took my pen in hand and began to write, in words that were to become immortal:

"I wish to become a teacher because I love children. The poet Robert Louis Stevenson said, 'The world is so full of a number of things/That I'm sure we should all be as happy as kings....' "

2
A Tale of Three Teachers

At the time I was aspiring to become a teacher, I had four hurdles to leap. The first was graduation from an accredited college with a bachelor's degree in education. The second hurdle was a four-hour written examination given by the Board of Education of the City of Chicago, pretending to assess the amount of pertinent information I had accumulated during those college years. The third obstacle was an oral exam; and the fourth, a cursory once-over by a Board physician, who had decided long ago in his career that if a candidate could survive the first three hurdles, he deserved to pass the fourth.

The most feared of the four was the oral exam. Put that way, "oral exam," it might sound to the uninitiate as though we candidates had to line up, open wide, and say "ahhhh" while the Board dentist examined the state of our gums or counted the number of teeth extant. Not that they didn't do that, too, but that came later, as part of the physical exam.

The orals were the inquisitorial trial to which we were invited *if* we passed the written examination. For the orals, we were summoned downtown to the 228 Building and there called in one at a time to face a panel of six or seven sober-faced educators—principals mostly—who were there to rate us on such things as personality, poise, articulation, and an intangible quality called "teacher material." These panel members were forearmed; they had in front of them our college records, our scores from our written exams, and reports from our critic teachers.

We had been cautioned to be honest and straightforward in our replies. Supposedly, the examiners would be turned off by a know-it-all attitude, since they were veteran teachers who could see right through affectation or cocky self-assurance.

"If you don't know the answer, say so!" warned Dr. Adams, an education professor. "They will give you credit for candor, at any rate. And if you don't know, but think you know where or how to find out, tell them so. It may earn you a point or two for resourcefulness."

We all had a pretty good idea who would fail the orals for sure. There was the belligerent, antisocial classmate, whose clothes were always thickly matted with dog hairs. And the three-hundred pound young woman with a hearing disability, a booming voice, and the language of a longshoreman. There were moments, too, when we feared that during our own oral exams some psychological deviance would be uncovered that would forever bar us from the career for which we had been preparing so long and so earnestly.

The Board members had a bag of tricks. They knew our weaknesses and lost no time in attacking the vulnerable tendons. A friend of mine, talented but with a low frustration point, was asked to recite the first verse of "The Star Spangled Banner." Not *sing*, which she could have done easily, but *recite*. I know very few people who can do it. *I* can't. She couldn't, either, and she broke down and cried. Her points dropped accordingly.

A bright young history buff, who was a notoriously poor speller, was sent to the chalkboard for a test. "Confederate," "Soviet Socialist Republic," and "Massachusetts" sent him back to his seat, demoralized.

Applicants who had made poor scores in the grammar section of the written test were sent to the board to diagram sentences—and failed.

Most of the questions addressed to me dealt with classroom management and discipline, perhaps because the Board sensed that those were potential areas of

17

weakness for me. (They most certainly *were* during my first three days of teaching!)

I clung to Dr. Adam's admonitions as closely as I could. "Be honest! Be humble!" She hadn't ruled out adroitness, however, so I parried. I prefaced my answers candidly with "This is how my critic teacher handled an incident like that, and I think I would do the same—" Or, "My critic teacher has had great success with this technique, and I plan on trying it myself—" Or, "My critic teacher has settled that problem once and for all by doing such and such—"

I kept up this artful dodging for some time; after all, what does a student teacher who is never left alone with a class know about discipline?

Finally the interview ended, and Dr. Rafferty, the head of the Board of Examiners, said he had one more question to put to me—off the record.

"If I asked you what kind of teacher you'd like to be, would your answer be 'Just like my critic teacher'?" Without giving me a chance to answer, he went on, "And, by the way, what is the name of this phenomenal teacher?"

I was most fortunate in having as a critic one of the three most "phenomenal" teachers I have ever known. When I remember Helen Baldry now, it is not so much as my mentor, but as an unforgettable person—a slayer of rattlesnakes, a tatter of exquisite lace, a wilderness camper and Girl Scout leader, a collector of fine china and sterling, and a most remarkable human being.

I first met Helen on a tour of the Billings School with Lucille, my sidekick. Lucille and I were slated to put in approximately five months of practice teaching at the Billings, and on this our first visit we were touring the classrooms and deciding which teachers we would like to work under. I liked Helen immediately, even though I was sure she was doing everything wrong. For one thing, she taught sitting down, and if we'd had anything drilled into us in methods courses it was to stand up where you could see and be seen. But Helen sat for the entire forty minutes, not at all embarrassed by our presence.

Helen was not a physically attractive person, although I soon forgot to notice what had struck me so forcefully at first—that there was something of the bulldog about her, in her heavily-jowled face, in the thrust of her head, in the manner in which she braced herself, arms akimbo on the desk in order to shift her weight from time to time.

Far more intriguing than her appearance was her rapport. The pupils didn't seem as put off by Helen's entrenchment behind her desk as I was. With few exceptions, they hung on her words, and when she threw out questions, the kids responded enthusiastically. She never praised a correct answer, and she frequently shot down the giver of a foolish reply. I was momentarily shocked, until I noticed that it didn't disturb the youngsters at all; they bounced back for a second chance to answer correctly and more to the point. (Years later, when I saw "The Paper Chase" on TV and enjoyed the acerbic professor, I said to my family, "There's Helen! That's her technique!")

Helen spoke in cultured tones, her enunciation precise, but there was a noticeable tremor in her voice. The combination of sitting while teaching, the quavering voice, and the frizzy, unstyled permanent led me to believe that she was twenty to twenty-five years my senior. That first day in her class I had a transient, unworthy thought that she was close to retirement and maybe I would have a chance at her job. It was a vain aspiration; she had another fifteen years of teaching in her.

When I asked Helen that day if she would be my critic teacher the next semester, she responded graciously. And when she discovered that English was my minor, she said enthusiastically, "Good! English is not exactly my forte." I think she truly meant that, but I learned in a semester under her guidance that there was no area in which she did not show expertise. I learned also why she sat most of the time; she was arthritic—badly so—and sitting spared her a great deal of pain. However, if the occasion called for it—if Tom stuck his foot into the aisle to trip Betsy on her way back to her desk—Helen could be out of her seat in a flash, lift the offender by the ear while he was still smirking over his achievement, and have him sitting on the floor at her side, back braced against the drawers of her desk, effectively removed from the attention of his peers before those in the last few seats were able to piece it all together.

I discovered, too, that Helen sponsored the school paper and spent most of her lunch hours supervising the typing of articles, as well as the layout. And when the paper was out of the way, she busied herself in other projects, like setting up the hand looms for her students.

Helen was a perfectionist, demanding a lot from her children and more from herself. There were always written homework assignments.

"Aren't you ever tempted to throw them all out?" I asked her one day, watching her red-pencil through forty history reports. I should have known better than to ask.

"They took the time to write these; the least I can do is correct them," was her cryptic reply.

There have been nights since that time, when I was teaching high school, that I have remembered Helen's integrity and splashed cold water over my burning eyes, reached for a cold can of soda, and resisted the temptation to throw the lot of them—sixty to ninety compositions a week—into the incinerator.

Ignoring her crippling disease, Helen made an exquisite graduation dress for a motherless student. The graduate's younger sister gave away the secret, telling how the two of them, Miss Baldry and Karen, went from shop to shop looking at the various styles, trying them on for size, and then selecting a pattern and material; and how Helen spent long evenings fashioning the gown in a labor of love.

Helen had an award system. The four highest ranking students were given a year-end treat. Most teachers I know, myself included, don't want to see anyone under twenty-one from the day school closes in June until it opens again in September, but Helen's award for good scholarship and citizenship was a weekend trip either to Hannibal, Missouri—Mark Twain's country—or Springfield, Illinois—Lincoln's home and tomb. Helen did the driving and picked up the tab for the weekend. Most remarkable of all, she did it *after* school was closed, when all of her friends were on guided tours in Scandinavia, the British Isles, or Greece.

I never did supplant Helen; I had grossly overestimated the difference in our ages, for one thing. But I did return to Billings and teach next door to her for several years, and then went on to a nearby high school. Soon after my last move, Helen died, suddenly and unexpectedly, and for weeks I was stopped almost daily in the halls by students who had known both of us at the Billings and who were having trouble—as I was—accepting the fact of her death. They would come up to me with incredulity or protest, or both, in their breaking voices, and tell me, "Hey, Mrs. Reichel, Miss Baldry is *dead!*" And I would reply, under the din of the passing students both for my comfort and for theirs, "I know. I miss her so much. But we were very lucky to have had her for a teacher. There'll never be another like her!"

Yes, I would like to have become a teacher like Helen Baldry.

Or like Louise Frye. Mrs. Frye taught in the primary grades at the Columbus School on the city's northwest side. The superlatives that come to mind when I think of this teacher are so overworked that they hardly seem adequate. She was energetic, enthusiastic, dedicated, and—above all—a woman of integrity and tremendous warmth.

For Martha, Tom, and Debby, our three oldest children, it was love at first sight as each of them—over a period of four years—entered Mrs. Frye's first-grade classroom. This grand passion of theirs had little to do with class excursions—to Brookfield Zoo in the fall, Marshall Field's at Christmas, Hawthorn-Melody Farms in the spring, Lincoln Park, fire stations, hospitals, and wherever else struck Mrs. Frye's fancy—even at a time when teachers were discouraged from such activities, because parents had suddenly discovered liability suits! No, it wasn't only her spirit of adventure. There was a charisma about her, a spell of enchantment that capti-

21

vated every one of her charges. She had love enough for them all, and they soaked it up like sponges, according to their need.

Debby's year with Mrs. Frye was frequently interrupted by hospital visits related to Debby's arthritis. Each time she was confined there were messages from the class, works of art designed by Mrs. Frye and executed by the children under her guidance. A year after Debby left Mrs. Frye's room, she was again hospitalized—this time around the Christmas season. A beautiful doll arrived at her bedside one morning from her former and still favorite teacher, Mrs. Frye.

Louise was loving and compassionate; she was also a superior teacher who enjoyed her work. I spoke to an education professor at Teachers College about what an impact she had made on my children. She cut me short with, "You can't tell me anything about Louise Frye that I don't already know. I take my K-Three methods classes over there every semester to let them observe her in action. She's tremendous!"

Mrs. Frye's devotion and conscientious work with the children was repaid by a fierce loyalty—at least in one case that I know of. A friend and I were supervising a department in a vacation Bible school in our neighborhood church. We had about a dozen primary children in our care, and during a lull, while the children were cutting and pasting, we began to talk about school in general and Mrs. Frye in particular. When we had exhausted our store of praise, I commented, "The most remarkable thing about it is that Louise Frye is black—the only black teacher in an all-white school."

A young boy at our table leaped up, overturning his chair and scattering his handwork in his excitement. His fists were doubled in anger, his face distorted and turning red. "Mrs. Frye is *not* black!" he shouted at us. "She's *not* black! She's *white!*"

We talked it over at the dinner table that night, that violent reaction of the young first-grader. Our children, after some discussion, agreed that somewhere along the way, Johnny had been taught that blacks were bad, and since he knew beyond a flicker of a doubt that Mrs. Frye was good, he figured she could not be black! We prayed that his heart would someday correct his prejudice.

Peter, my half-brother, was in Mrs. Frye's first-grade class a few years before our first child began school. In October, six-year-old Peter's father died suddenly.

"That little tyke broke my heart," Louise told me years later. "Every morning as soon as the children had settled down to work, Peter would wander up to my desk, and he'd look at me with those huge, forlorn brown eyes and say, 'My daddy died.' Every morning, for weeks, as though it had just happened the night before. All I could do was hug him and say, 'I know, Peter. I know.' That seemed to be all he needed. He'd go back to his desk and be all right for the rest of the day."

Helen Baldry and Louise Frye, two exceptional teachers.

And then there was Agnes Lytle.

Agnes was a feisty little Irish woman who taught sixth grade at the Knight School, my first successful assignment. Sixth grade was the highest level in our particular building, and the children ranged in age from eleven through fifteen. They were worldly-wise adolescents, most of them quite large for their age, towering over Agnes, who was a few inches under five feet. I had heard that she was an excellent teacher, but I was too busy establishing my own reputation to pay much attention to anyone else's—until I was forced to, during my second semester at Knight.

Agnes had contracted some strange malady that defied diagnosis and treatment, and she began taking an occasional day off to rest. Gradually her illness worsened, and she would be away for days at a time. I sat in my room during the lunch hour one day when a young man—handsome, sharply attired, and of quarterback proportions—entered and introduced himself as Miss Lytle's substitute. I made some polite, welcoming sounds and waited for him to go on.

"When does it happen?" he asked.

"When does *what* happen?"

"When does the roof cave in?"

I stared at him uncomprehendingly.

23

"I have been in that classroom all morning, and nothing has happened yet," he said. There was no doubting the anxiety in his voice.

"What is supposed to happen?" I asked.

"They're setting me up for something," he explained. "All morning it's been 'Yes, Mr. Jones,' 'No, Mr. Jones,' 'May I please use the dictionary, Mr. Jones?' 'Thank you, Mr. Jones.' No one talks out of turn. No one's thrown anything. If they drop anything, they pick it up. Nobody's tried to start a fight. Are they waiting for the dismissal bell at three fifteen? Is that when they'll all break loose?"

"Mr. Jones, just relax and enjoy the rest of the day. Nothing's going to happen. Not in Miss Lytle's class. And don't ask me why."

He left, not at all convinced.

Miss Lytle was going to be out the entire week, and Mr. Jones promised to return the next day, Tuesday, but he would not commit himself any farther ahead than that. When he signed out on Tuesday, he told the clerk he would come in on Wednesday. And when Wednesday proved to be without incident, he stopped by to tell me so, jubilant and a foot off the ground.

On the fourth day, he left a sheaf of papers with me, compositions he had assigned to the class and which he had just finished reading. The topic was "The Person I Most Admire." Of the thirty-five or so compositions, all but two were about Agnes Lytle. The students had expressed in highly individualistic styles and terminology their love and respect for their teacher. What was evident in every paper was the pupils' conviction that their teacher had restored their self-respect, encouraged them to develop a sense of self-worth, and inspired them to conduct themselves like ladies and gentlemen—not only for her sake and in her presence alone, but for their own sakes and at all times. Only a teacher can appreciate what an incredible accomplishment that was!

"If I asked you what kind of teacher you'd like to be, would your answer be 'Just like my critic teacher'?" the head of the Board of Examiners had asked me over twenty years ago. I had enough sense then to recognize that Helen Baldry was a superb teacher, and the years of experience since then have only strengthened my original impression. But now from my vantage point of experience and time, I have to place alongside Helen's name that of Louise Frye, who left such a deep impression on my family with her loving concern. And Agnes Lytle, with her gift for imparting dignity and her decision to remain in the inner city, where that gift was so desperately needed.

From those three I learned that the ultimate success of a teacher is not dependent on academic preparation—as necessary as it may be—but on his or her own character. These are the teachers whose children rise up and call them blessed.

Everett, looking over my shoulder again, says, "As long as you're immortalizing teachers, don't forgot Eleanor Donovan, from Elkland, Pennsylvania, my high school English teacher!" And Everett, who has to phone me from the Beach Road Market, two miles from home, to find out what it was he was supposed to pick up, can still recite, "The boy stood on the burning deck. Whence all but he had fled. . ." and other selections drilled into him by the ambitious Miss Donovan almost sixty years ago.

No, Everett, I won't forget Miss Donovan. She helped you get rid of your double negatives and taught you that your verbs had to agree with their subjects in number. If she hadn't, I probably wouldn't have given you a second look when our paths crossed forty years ago in a Chicago mission!

3
First Time Out

"Let's not cry here," I pleaded with Lucille as we settled ourselves in the front seat of her battered DeSoto. She nodded, fumbled with her keys, finally found the ignition, and maneuvered the car out of the school parking lot. She drove north for a couple of blocks until we were safely ahead of the 1500 kids streaming from the fortress-type plant. A few minutes later, she pulled out of the Division Street traffic and parked. Making sure the doors were locked, we sat back and let the tears come.

We were too old to cry—too old by a whole generation—but that didn't deter us. How old is *too* old? I was admitting to thirty-seven, and Lucille was pushing fifty. Far beyond the age, both of us, when weeping can be done with grace—and without aftermath. Nevertheless we huddled there on that cold January afternoon, sobbing with abandon, oblivious to the curious stares of occasional passers-by. Let them think what they wished. We had reason to lament. Our hearts were broken—our spirits lacerated—our aspirations in the dust. What should have been one of the happiest times of our lives had turned into a frightening fiasco.

A week before, we had been graduated from Chicago Teachers College, part of the first harvest of overage college drop-ins. A bit uncomfortable in our caps, gowns, and bifocals, Lucille and I had marched self-consciously down the aisle as our children—seven between the two of us—watched from the sidelines. We held our mortared heads high, however, because out of that class of 125 we were the only ones who had jobs waiting for us on the outside. Our fellow classmates would have to serve six-week stints as substitute teachers before being offered assignments. So there was a smugness to the swing of our tassels, a brave attempt at humility in our expressions; and if our incredible naiveté was showing, no one had the heart to tell us.

It had all begun the day before commencement, when the two of us were singled out and approached by a talent scout—a young and aggressive elementary school principal on her way up to a district superintendency—who had just been placed in charge of a model experimental school. It seemed she had chosen us not so much for our respectable academic records as for our gray hairs. "Maturity" was the term of entrapment she used. "I want mature women, who know what they're about," she confided, leaning forward the better to see our credentials: liver spots, crow's feet, dewlaps. We were intrigued by the realization that advanced age could be a marketable asset.

"There will be a few drawbacks," young Dr. Conway cautioned us over lunch at Boling's (*her* treat) in the Board of Education building. "Our brand new facility is not yet completed, and you will have to rough it—just temporarily, of course—at the Jamison School. Only for a few weeks—" Her voice faded out, but returned again more vigorously as she mentioned some of the innovations awaiting us in the new building.

"Closed circuit TV, a modern audio-visual center, beautiful cafeteria—the eyes of the whole educational world upon you." Her sales pitch had me enthralled. I couldn't wait to go home and tell my family, "See, it's just as I've always told you! The rewards of clean living and burning the midnight oil *are* fame and fortune!" In the meantime I tried to send a silent message to Lucille: "Aren't we the lucky ones?" But Lucille was carefully avoiding any eye contact, mine or Dr. Conway's. She was painstakingly concentrating on buttering a corn muffin.

"Of course," Dr. Conway continued, her voice again dropping to a conspiratorial pitch, "supplies might be short until we can make the move from the Jamison to the new building—" She cleared her throat and dismissed that contingency with a renewed expression of confidence.

"I'm sure that you two women, having been mothers and all, will be most resourceful."

I nodded enthusiastically, emboldened by her faith. I was positive at that point that I could climb any mountain, storm any bastion, and out-resource any teacher in the Chicago public schools. In the meantime, with trembling hands, I clumsily cleared a space on the crowded table, tipping over a glass of water in the process, to make room for the contracts that Dr. Conway had removed from her attaché case.

For a homebound housewife who hadn't signed anything of any significance since I had raised my right hand eighteen years before at the marriage license bureau, this was an exhilarating business. I found myself intoxicated by the calculated headiness of the environment—my first exposure to the 228 Building on a professional basis, elbow-rubbing with the "Downtown Personnel," and first-name intimacy in the elevators.

Lucille's fervor did not match mine. She ignored the papers awaiting our signatures. Simultaneously kicking my ankle with the toe of her pointed pump and pushing herself away from the table, she said, "Before we sign, I think we ought to visit the Jamison and see what our 'temporary situation' will be." Granted, she spoke with the proper deference, with a certain winsome hesitancy, a "no offense is intended" posture, but she embarrassed me, nevertheless. Her lack of trust—indeed, her lack of reverence—I could only attribute to the fact that Lucille was the mother of one teacher and the wife of another—a case in point of contempt bred by familiarity.

Dr. Conway was obviously annoyed by Lucille's balk, and when she canceled our dessert, pineapple cheesecake, in order to drive us to the Jamison, so was I. Annoyed, I mean.

My petulance evaporated at my first glimpse of the

Jamison. There is something in me that loves old buildings, finds romance in crumbling plaster and scarred woodwork, and is entranced by shadowy halls inhabited by ghosts of generations past. Therefore I was undaunted and thrilled by the ugly architecture of the nineteenth-century edifice. I figured that its institutional odors, its foreboding murkiness, and its Stygian aspect were in character with its Victorian origins. What's more, I had the exalted—and condescending—conviction that I could bring to these benighted corridors something illuminating and inspirational. In a word, myself.

Sharing neither my altruism nor my literary leanings, Lucille's first impressions were far different. She was a pragmatic science-math major and consequently took note of such items as the number of students per classroom, the condition of the duplicating machines, the number of boarded-up windows, and the inadequate lighting. While I was groveling in sentimentality, she was locating the teachers' lounge, tallying the teacher-absence total for the day by surreptitiously peeking at the sign-in sheets, and establishing rapport with the head clerk.

Our tour guide, Dr. Conway, kept our dallying to a minimum, whisked us over the premises, introduced us to persons in authority, and at frequent intervals reminded us that the Jamison was to be only a temporary home. Before we could catch our breath, she had us back in her car and was uncapping her fountain pen for a second time. Lucille and I suppressed any misgivings we may have had and surrendered our signatures. Later, I was to blame my capitulation on temporary madness. Lucille's defense was that she felt so "obligated"—the dinner at Boling's, Dr. Conway's insistence that she take an hour from her busy schedule to conduct us personally through the Jamison, and above all, the bonus of being "chosen."

That Thursday we signed our contracts, and on Monday we reported for work. And here it was Wednesday—three days into our new teaching careers—and we sat in Lucille's car near the intersection of Division and Elston, sobbing our hearts out.

29

"I can't go back," Lucille blubbered into her scarf.

"Neither can I," I whimpered.

"It's asking too much—" she began, only to collapse over the steering wheel in a paroxysm of weeping.

"We won't go back!" I declared, consolingly, recklessly, between convulsive breaths.

"But we signed a contract!" Lucille wailed.

"They can tear up the contract!" I hiccupped, cavalierly tossing away four years of hard-wrested college education, of tasteless frozen dinners, vacationless summers, and the blind faith of my husband and four children.

"I'm quitting!" I reiterated. "At least," I amended, "I'm going to call Dr. Conway and tell her I want out."

"You wouldn't dare!" Lucille challenged hopefully.

"Oh, yes, I would!"

She was quiet while I mopped up and powdered over my damaged areas. I was pretty sure I knew what was going through her mind. She was probably thinking about her husband, an assistant principal, and her son, a physical education teacher. Would reneging result in retaliation? Would her family be blacklisted? I had heard stories, unsubstantiated but frightening, of the "system" and how it took care of its own. Well, I decided disloyally, that was *her* problem. As for me, *I* had no relatives who would be purged if I defected.

"Tell Dr. Conway we *both* want out," Lucille choked. I nodded solemnly. We were joined in a professional suicide pact.

Lucille and I had not known each other before Teachers College. There we became linked together by the accident of last names that were so identical that nobody could ever squeeze between us alphabetically. We were seated next to each other in the classes that we shared. We were sent to the same pleasant, middle-class school for our semester of practice teaching; and although we were exact physical opposites—Lucille had a fashionable lean and hungry look, and I did not—we good-humoredly accepted being called by the other's name. It was inevitable that we should both be recommended for the Jamison Experiment. Perhaps our college counselor assumed that we would support one another when the going got intolerable, and thus survive. But it didn't work out that way.

We lasted three days in the belly of that behemoth the Jamison School, thus fulfilling the prophecy of Rosella, one of my third graders.

"Teachuh," she asked, before I could even introduce myself to the class, "how long you gonna stay? We ain't had no teachuh stay mo' den three days."

Another pupil eagerly corroborated her boast. "We done had nine teachuhs since Chris'mus," he assured me happily that third week in January.

The poor waifs, I sympathized silently. *Innocent victims of unfaithful, undedicated, uncaring, day-to-day substitutes. Well, things will be different from this point on.* I gazed at them with a look of love. I smiled at every one of the forty-eight tykes, and to disarm them further I took Rosella's hand and squeezed it gently.

"You won't get rid of me that easily," I promised. "I'm going to be your teacher until school is out in June."

I misinterpreted the riotous response as enthusiasm. "*Amor* does *vincit omnia!*" I gloated, convinced I had won them over already. I was mistaken. They were not applauding my winsome approach; they were hooting at my naiveté. Some were even making wagers as to my staying power. A few prognosticators had me leaving before recess. None expected me back the next morning.

As I waited for the hubbub to fade, I had time to recall the words of Helen, my critic teacher and mentor, as I stumbled through my five months of internship. Only a week before, she had handed me a list of "don'ts" that she said would guarantee my success. The first negative suggestion on the list was "Don't smile for the first three months," and here I was, three months ahead of schedule.

When the children finally quieted down to find out what direction my next *faux pas* would take, I called the roll. Rapidly. I finished—out of breath, but without incident. The anticipatory hush hung on. The still small

31

voice of my mentor advised me: "Now's the time to crack the whip! Put them to work before they know what's hit them. And for Pete's sake, don't talk too much!"

I brushed the phantom voice aside and gave in to a stronger, self-destructive, fool-rushing-in urge. *Now's the time to establish rapport,* I decided. Only ten minutes into my first day of solo teaching, and I was about to make my second serious mistake!

Leaning informally against the desk, feigning nonchalance, I began to narrate the story of my life, convinced those third-graders would be interested in my children, my pets, and—most of all—my desire to lead them out of the ghetto into a world "so full of a number of things."

They could not have cared less. They interrupted my monologue with every request imaginable, irrelevant and profane comments, and personal and insolently intimate queries that brought a blush to my cheek and forced me to abandon my attempt at rapping. Too late I decided to shut my mouth and proceeded to distribute the supplies I had brought with me. Catcalls and imprecations followed me down the aisles. I clenched my jaws and wheeled the portable and miserably inadequate chalkboard to the front of the room. On the board were ten problems I had placed there earlier.

There was an instant change in the character of the din; it took on the ominous sound of a revolution.

"Do these problems," I shouted over the noisy rebellion. "And do them neatly," I warned. To my relief some of the children began to copy the figures. There was a gradual, if sullen, capitulation. Gratified, I patroled the aisles and praised the neat columns, checked their headings, and kept repeating, "Neatly, please," hoping it would slow them down.

The majority of the children were finished in fifteen minutes. I collected the papers and glanced nervously at my watch. Only 9:30! I sent a note across the hall to where Lucille was entrenched with her class. "How long until recess?" I wrote.

Her answer came back, quickly and cryptically: "*Too long!*"

I derived a measure of comfort from her implied anguish, guessing—nay, hoping—that she was in similar straits. My misery craved company.

I sighed and took out my *Arbuthnot Anthology*, telling the children they had worked so well that I would read to them until recess. They didn't applaud, but neither did they object. I began with Christopher Robin and Winnie the Pooh—universal favorites, I thought. Well, A. A. Milne may have been popular in Buckingham Palace and in my own parlor, but he bombed at the Jamison. They listened—I'll grant them that—but they were unmoved.

I turned next to a Scandinavian folk tale about Goody Gudrun and her impractical horse-trading husband, but before I could finish, Rosella, whom I had now identified as the spokesman for the class, complained, "How many of them dumb stories we gotta listen to, Teachuh?"

Her official second piped up, "Yeah, Teachuh. Ain't you got no bettuh book?"

I slapped the book shut, ordered them to put their heads down on their desks for a rest, and wrote another note to Lucille. "What are you doing?" I scribbled, hoping for a constructive reply.

The note came back, amended to read: "What are you doing here?" Below that she had scrawled, "You tell *me!*"

Clearly, there would be no help from that quarter. I passed out the last of my paper. Then, erasing the arithmetic problems, I printed in their place a list of spelling words. Remembering the quick work the children had made of the arithmetic assignment, I added five more words to the ten I had prepared. By the time I had finished, three fist fights had broken out, several bottles of chocolate milk had been spilled—Rosella had taken it upon herself to pass out the morning repast while my back was turned—and a fresh insurrection seemed imminent, judging from the increased volume of noise.

"Write each word five times!" I shouted over the din. For one fleeting, guilty moment I remembered my methods class in language arts: motivation, example, drill, culminating activity, and so on. My conscience suffered a feeble spasm, and I raised my voice again.

"And when you've finished writing them five times, *print* them five times." I guess I overreached. Rosella rebelled while the class watched.

"I ain't gonna write all them dumb words all them times!" She sat back with folded arms, murder in her eye. The rest of the children followed their leader.

In an atavistic reaction I picked up the yardstick and approached the desk of the multi-plaited rebel.

"Say that again," I ordered. "I'm not sure I heard you correctly." I slapped the stick against my leg as I advanced toward Rosella. My menacing expression concealed a most devout and desperate interior. "Please, Lord, let me have this round," I prayed.

Rosella's arms relaxed, but her fists remained ready for action.

"Effen I does do it," she threatened, "it'll take me all day."

"That's fine with me," I replied, more heartily than I had intended. Rosella began her spelling with an exaggerated slowness, and the others followed suit. It appeared I was going to have a respite of sorts. The sweet taste of even this small success engendered a feeling of magnanimity. I sent a message to Lucille. "Try brandishing a yardstick," I advised.

"I brandished mine already," she replied, "and let me tell you, two 18-inch segments are not as effective as one 36-inch one. May I borrow yours?"

Before I could refuse, the relative quiet of the room was broken by the ringing of a double bell. This was followed by a cacaphony of cheers. I beat a tattoo on Rosella's desk and demanded silence. I settled for a slight reduction in din.

"That's the recess bell," I informed them. "And as soon as I can hear a pin drop, I'll let you get your wraps and—"

Oh, the hooting that erupted! The pounding on the desks and the stomping on the floor that ensued!

"What a stoopid teachuh! We don' need no wraps to go to the toilet!"

"What kinda school you come fum, Teachuh? Don' you know a indoor recess bell when you hears one?"

A message from Lucille shored me up: "I'll take the boys, if you'll take the girls."

That was good of her, I thought. *Choosing the more obstreperous sex.*

"Let's get this over with as quickly as possible," I said to the girls as I escorted them down the hall. "Then you'll have longer to play." I fully expected them to comply. After all, it was in their best interests to do so.

In retrospect, I believe my biggest mistake in that first journey to the loo was leaving my yardstick behind me. I had missed it immediately as I stepped into the hall, but there wasn't time to return for it. I was too busy trotting after the kids as they raced down the corridors. I assumed their haste was physiological in origin. In a way it was. They had a surprise in store for me, and they were in a hurry to show it.

How strange that in all my years of attending school and in my semester of practice teaching I had never seen the possibility of the lavatory doubling as a jungle gym. I watched in fascinated horror as the girls stormed the washroom, used the toilet bowls as stepping stones to the horizontal framework around the stalls, chinned themselves, hung by their knees and pulled their phizzogs into ghastly inverted masks. Those who were not working out on the bars ran around flushing toilets, opening faucets, stopping up sink drains, fist fighting, and name-calling.

I plunged into the melee and collared two of the smaller ones. I took them back into the hall and told them to stay put. "Or else!" I threatened, leaving the consequences to their imagination. I waded back in for a second pair and added them to my reluctant exiles. I kept this up until it dawned on me that I was getting nowhere; the number of girls in the hall remained constant. They were slipping back into the washroom as fast as I was dragging them out!

A bell rang, heralding the end of indoor recess—and just in time. I was on the point of tears. Immediately the bedlam ceased, and of their own volition the girls

The lavatory doubled as a jungle gym.

abandoned the scene of their rascality and followed me almost docilely back to the room.

Lucille had my boys lined up quietly outside the classroom door. She took one look at my flushed, disheveled self and whispered, "Next time send them in four at a time. If they don't come out promptly, the next four can't go in. Peer pressure, remember?"

Well, it was all right for her to talk; she could easily beat the kids in a footrace down the hall. I would need a sixty-second head start. I turned my resentment against Lucille and my humiliation at my defeat toward the kids as soon as we were all back in the room with the door shut. A few had taken up their pencils to continue with the spelling assignment. I picked up my yardstick, which was fast becoming my symbol of authority, and ordered them to stop working.

I began another impassioned lecture, telling them how I had been looking forward to coming to their school. Exercising a little poetic license, I described the better schools I might have chosen, explaining how I had opted for this particular place because I wanted to help them pick themselves up by their bootstraps.

It was the same introductory speech they had tuned out earlier that morning, only now it was heavy with emotion and based on experience. I strode up and down the aisles, punctuating my sentences with raps on the desks, affectionate rubbing of frizzy pates, and the squeezing of scrawny shoulders. There was a brink-of-tears huskiness in my voice that heightened the effect of my presentation. They were spellbound. So was I. I realized that I "had" them now.

Well, for a while. I *had* discovered how to turn them on, and in the three days that I was to spend in their midst I would have to resort to my demonstrative monologue a half-dozen times in order to quell rebellion. It was inevitable that my delivery would lose its punch and my voice its timbre.

Lunch hour finally came that first day, and I spent it trying to put together an afternoon program that would work. Lucille spent the noon hour scrounging in unlocked classrooms. About 2:00 P.M., when a music lesson collapsed, I wrote her another note. "Now what are you doing?" I asked, not so much from a need to know as from a need to know she was still there.

"I got hold of some clay, and we're working with that," she replied.

"Have you got any extra?" I scribbled.

"Yes," she replied, "but I strongly advise against it."

I didn't insist. Intuition and five hours of experience gave me an indication as to what she might be going through.

At 3:30 I led my children out of the building. While I preceded the class, those in the rear took advantage of the opportunity, demolishing the valentine bulletin board I had constructed early that morning. Returning to my room for my wraps, I fought back the tears and cleaned up the pink crepe paper and crumpled velvet ribbons.

We counted our losses on the ride home. We were depressed, but we rallied somewhat and planned our strategies for the next day. We took comfort in Lucille's discovery that we did have recourse to a teacher/disciplinarian, a Mr. Sharpe. Lucille had been told by another teacher, "When the situation gets really rough, send for Mr. Sharpe."

On our second day, between the two of us, we sent for Mr. Sharpe a total of nine times. My first two frantic calls were answered within minutes. The third call took a little longer. My fourth went unanswered for an hour.

But the veteran teacher was right about one thing. Mr. Sharpe had only to walk into the room, and a convulsive shiver would pass through the class. Whatever bedlam had been taking place came to an abrupt halt when this slightly-built, humorless legend appeared; whichever kids were out of their seats would scramble back to home base and sit tall, hands folded and faces bug-eyed. He didn't say anything. He just stood there and stared at the children, who seemed to suspend their breathing in his presence. I felt almost as threatened as the kids when he was in the room, and I was glad to see him leave, even though I learned after that first visit that pandemonium would resume as soon as he left.

38

"Why are you so good when Mr. Sharpe comes to visit?" I asked.

Rosella's eyes rolled expressively. "'Cuz he whups us!"

"And he throws us in the wastebasket upside down," Horatio added, pointing to the three-foot-high container.

"And makes us stay there until our eyeballs pop!" someone else volunteered.

By the third day the situation took on an uglier tone. Openly disappointed at our return, the children redoubled their efforts in what was obviously a campaign to force us out. They had seen our bag of tricks, and now they wanted to make way for the next act. They began the morning by bombarding me with requests to visit the washroom, knowing it was not permitted except in special cases. Rosella, the first to ask, did not attempt to hide her glee when I refused permission.

"OK, Teachuh! Effen you won't let me go to the washroom, I'll wet my pants." And she proceeded to do so. Others followed her example throughout the day. After the fourth or fifth accident-on-purpose, I stopped sending for the janitor.

The children made no attempt to do any of the work I assigned. The paper I passed out was thrown on the floor, but not before it was covered with obscenities. The cartons of milk delivered before recess and heretofore emptied hungrily were now sacrificed to the cause, spilled over desks and floors and neighbors.

I began to write a final, desperate plea to Mr. Sharpe. Rosella, from her front-row seat informed me dispassionately, "Teachuh, dat ain't gonna do no good. Mr. Sharpe ain't gonna come no more. He done been here enuf."

Lucille sent me a note just before noon, asking me to meet her in the office with my class roster. She was waiting for me, her appearance a haggard and exhausted reflection of mine—with one difference. There was an air of purposefulness about her posture. I followed her to a side room where the student folders were kept. There she told me what we were up to.

We were going to check the folders of each of our pupils to find out how many had blue slips stapled to their records, indicating that a psychological study had been made of that child. As we rapidly flicked through the files, the significance of our discovery was staggering. Every one of our ninety-six or more children had been blue-slipped. Every one at some point in his or her young life had exhibited the type of deviate behavior that prompted the classroom teacher to keep an anecdotal account and to request outside help. The blue slip did not divulge the nature of the child's problem; it was merely a reminder that, in the confidential files in the counselor's office—under lock and key—were the results of that study.

Lucille, the pragmatic science major, was not finished. She had brought two more third grade rosters, borrowed from assigned Jamison teachers. Those were classes that would be staying on at the Jamison, not moving into the model school a few blocks away, Dr. Conway's experimental school. "Now let's check these," Lucille ordered.

As we went through the second sets of files, we uncovered the conspiracy. Only two or three of those ninety-plus children had been blue-slipped. It was evident that someone had unloaded on us, the interim teachers, as many of the disturbed third graders as they could fit into our two classes. In other words, the opening of the experimental school was a beautiful opportunity for the Jamison administration to jettison their troublemakers.

I should have felt only dismay, I suppose. Instead, I was genuinely relieved. Now I could say, "No wonder!" Now I could get out from under the conviction that I was simply ineffectual in the classroom. I remarked almost cheerfully, "Well, that puts a different light on the situation. It should be all downhill from here on."

"What are you talking about?" demanded Lucille.

"We'll start pinching a few scapulars, tweaking some ears, and dumping the kids in the wastebaskets—upside down," I said, only half joking.

"You don't seem to understand," she wailed. "We don't have a hope!"

She was right, of course. The problem was more serious than I wanted to admit. Lucille soon made it clear that the ratio of forty-eight emotionally disturbed children to one soon-to-be emotionally disturbed teacher augured nothing but disaster. I returned to my room in a bleaker mood than ever, my feet and spirits dragging.

The children were jubilant, however, and couldn't wait to shuck their wraps and get to work on me. The incidents that afternoon trebled; the kids had a record to uphold, and they set about making sure I would not want to return for a fourth day. The same kind of bedlam reigned across the hall in Lucille's room. The noise carried through two closed doors.

That was the day we sat in the car and wept, and that was the night I phoned Dr. Conway and described our ordeal.

"It's an intolerable situation!" I cried, unable to hold back a sob.

"But you women signed a contract," she reminded me. "Surely you can hold on for a few weeks until we move to the new building."

I told her about Lucille's hunch, our lunch hour detective work, and the sickening discovery we had made. My recital was a painful one, because in the telling I became aware that Lucille and I were not the only ones who had been victimized. Something highly unethical had been going on behind the scenes, and Dr. Conway and her experimental school were the real losers.

There was a long, uncomfortable silence after I finished, while Dr. Conway absorbed the information. Whatever she was experiencing—betrayal, humiliation, or anger—she certainly couldn't share it with me, a probationary teacher. But when she spoke again the sharpness was gone from her voice. "Don't worry. I'll tear up your contracts," she promised. "You won't have to go back." Hesitating a moment, she added graciously, "I'm sorry. I'm terribly sorry that you were exposed to such an experience."

Our paths, Lucille's and mine, diverged almost immediately, once we joined the ranks of substitutes. We did a lot of telephoning back and forth for a couple of years for mutual comfort and advice, but our friendship gradually deteriorated to a Christmas card relationship, with infrequent reunions. Neither of us liked to talk about our "first time out"—perhaps because it was our first failure, at a time when we had thought we were invincible.

I like to think, whenever I recall the Jamison experience, that both of us would have performed admirably had we been given convenient chalkboards to send the children to and textbooks from which to make assignments. We had not been given a course in survival training for wasteland classrooms; rather, we had been trained in idealistic situations, where books and supplies were abundant and the only thing in short supply was the space in which to store them. Our cadeting had been done in rooms with reading corners, science tables, a piano, fifty feet of chalkboard, and—at our elbows, to keep us from falling on our faces—the omnipresent critic teachers.

But it is the Lord who directs my path, and He sent me to the Jamison—not so much to teach, perhaps, as to learn. I have come finally to look back upon those three days as a short course in humility. Those were the days when humility was a virtue worth praying for and that one could learn it only by being brought to the very end of oneself and to complete dependency upon God—the days before we got caught up in the traps of "consciousness raising," searching for the "real me," "getting it all together," and convincing oneself that "I'm OK, too"—the days when the emphasis was on the fact that as Christians "we live and move and exist" in Christ (Acts 17:28).

I well knew the warning "Pride goes before destruction" (Proverbs 16:18). But it took me a little longer to learn that "before honor comes humility" (Proverbs 15:33).

4
Clout

Having walked away from a crash-landing on my first teaching assignment, I decided that the most judicious move was to return to the classroom as quickly as possible—as a substitute. Everett agreed. My children, having had firsthand experience in the care and treatment of substitute teachers, did not. Tom, a veteran of three and a half years in a boys' high school, warned, "It's always open season on substitutes!"

"You haven't got a chance," Martha prognosticated dolefully.

"Maybe we ought to tell her what to watch out for," Debby offered.

"I don't think you should," their father warned. "Tell *me* instead."

I covered my ears and fled their presence, determined to hang onto my ignorance as long as I could. I went ahead and phoned the sub center and told them: "I am ready. You may call me any time."

Because there was a teacher shortage, I was sent out every day for five weeks to pinch-hit for teachers suffering from occupational disabilities: migraine, lower-back pain, and simple battle fatigue. For five weeks I endured a training in survival that put to shame the unrealistic methods courses required for a B.Ed. degree. However, and alas, like most experiences of any consequence in my life, that apprenticeship period proved to be better appreciated in retrospect than *in situ*.

43

In the six-weeks interim following graduation from Teachers College, I had progressed steadily from tribulation to patience to experience—and now I was living in expectation, as were all my fellow graduates. Our light at the end of the tunnel was the form letter from the Board, requesting our appearance in the personnel office for the purpose of being assigned.

The anticipation was almost unbearable. I longed desperately and hungrily for the trappings associated with being a "real" teacher. I wanted my own nylon-snagging desk; my personal mailbox in the main office, overflowing with directives and counter-directives, bulletins and glossy ads addressed to "Fourth Grade Teacher," a ring of keys to carry in my purse—for the classroom, the closets, and the faculty washroom—and above all, a little respect—the kind that goes with being a native of the territory and not merely a transient.

So when the summons finally arrived, I demanded a celebration.

"Let's all go out for dinner!" Everett suggested. There was unanimous agreement, and that night the six of us piled into the station wagon, bound for my victory banquet. We were a giddy and hilarious crew: I, because my emancipation was at hand; the kids, because there would be no kitchen chores; and Everett, because he had a surprise in store—our destination.

"This is not exactly what I had in mind!" I objected, as Everett swung into the MacDonald's parking lot.

He shrugged. "On such short notice, I couldn't get reservations at the Pump Room."

"And the Board of Health closed down your favorite hot dog stand," teased one of the children.

"And I suppose the Milk Pail said they will accept no substitutes, only assigned teachers." I sighed, conceding defeat. "Make mine a cheeseburger and a shake."

Later that evening, after exhausting my family's capacity for enthusiasm and in search of a fresh and more responsive audience, I decided to phone a few of my colleagues. It was an understandable urge, but a devastating mistake.

"Placement is not an invitation to the White House!"

44

I was admonished by Dianne. "It's more like banishment to Siberia. You'll be wishing you were back substituting!"

"It is not a dubbing." Howard laughed, amused at my innocence. "It is the shaft." Perhaps to cushion the blow, he confided, "A few of us are strategyzing tonight at my place. Care to join us?"

"Strategyzing?" I wondered, but I held my peace and accepted the invitation. I'd have time enough when I got there to find out what the word meant.

An hour later, over coffee and bagels, I learned that strategyzing was an exercise in survival, consisting chiefly of the pooling of information—information obtained from our interrogations of established teachers, the unconscionable pumping of nieces and nephews and neighbors' offspring, and the scuttlebutt picked up while substituting. From this intelligence we proceeded to compile a blacklist: schools to shun, principals to avoid, and neighborhoods to steer clear of. I use "we" loosely; *I* was only guilty by association. All of the input was provided by my co-conspirators while I munched on bagels and marveled at their cunning. Intrigue is not my forte—as my daughter pointed out, when she attempted to teach me the rudiments of chess.

But my lack of participation did not deter the rest of the underground. Once they had assessed the paucity of my contacts and the depth of my ignorance, they regrouped, leaving me on the sidelines. I spent that historic evening by the fireplace, lolling in a wing chair, mesmerized by the dancing flames and the snapping logs, and happily oblivious to the machinations going on behind me.

The meeting broke up at midnight, and while we were sorting out our snow boots, some observant soul noted that I was still there and voiced a considerate afterthought: "Say, did anybody give Reichel a copy of the blacklist?"

I dismissed his concern with a wave of the hand and a nonchalant "Don't worry about it." And then, afraid that someone might insist on staying just to accommodate me, I went on to reassure them and to nip their

Over coffee and bagels, I learned that strategyzing was an exercise in survival.

charitable instincts in the bud, "I don't have as much to worry about as the rest of you. I have the first scheduled appointment, Monday at eight A.M., so I'll get first choice of any openings—" My voice trailed off. I didn't need the sudden, incredulous silence to alert me to the fact that my attempt at self-effacement had backfired.

"You mean *you're* the one who got the highest combined scores?" a skeptic asked in hushed tones.

I nodded and attempted to slip through their midst before resentment displaced unbelief, but Howard had hold of my arm.

"Nice to know she's not a *complete* yo-yo, isn't it?" he asked, thus restoring me to grace.

We parted in laughter, at my expense, but a small price to pay for an evening before the fire, bagels and coffee, and the encouraging predictions of my friends that I was *so* right; there was nothing for me to worry about. "No, sirree!"

This combination of congenital gullibility and failure to profit from past experiences has contributed more than once to my downfall. Therefore, at eight o'clock on the following Monday, I approached the receptionist in the Office of Personnel, sans blacklist, but psyched for success.

"Reichel?" the young lady asked familiarly, pausing a second with nail file at the ready. I nodded, accepting her recognition as my due, only slightly humbled at this point by the absence of a red carpet.

"In there," she pointed the file over her left shoulder. "First cubicle on your right." She ticked off my name from the top of a long list of potential assignees and resumed her manicure, dismissing and deflating me most economically.

I entered the counselor's office, an eight-by-eight, plant-infested "home-away-from-home." As I settled myself in a chair, I found I was facing a large, thumbtacked map of the city of Chicago, ruled off into school districts. A hennaed head appeared in the doorway, looked me over, decided I was the type that could be put on "hold," and crisply directed, "Study the map. The tacks represent vacancies. Select your school. I'll be

47

back in a minute. Just gotta have a cuppa coffee!" An arm and hand joined the noggin to pantomime a splitting headache. At a sympathetic nod from me, the apparition disappeared.

I approached the map warily, my eyes seeking home territory—the safe side of Chicago in which I had been born, bred, and educated—in which I hoped to live out the rest of my days. My heart plummeted. That portion of the map was a tackless plain! I permitted my eyes to stray across my predetermined perimeters: Chicago Avenue on the south, Kedzie on the east. Spying a solitary tack in the buffer zone, I leaned closer to read the name of the school. I recoiled in haste. It was the Jamison School, where Lucille and I had bombed after three days. Now, too late, I understood the frantic buzz session of the coffee and bagel strategists. I wondered if there was anything to be gained by tampering with the tacks, but the return of the counselor checked my criminal urge.

"Well," she gushed, obviously rejuvenated by her "cuppa." "What have you decided?" she asked.

I looked helplessly from her to the map and back again remembering my optimistic "Don't worry about me. I'll have first choice—" "First refusal" would have been more accurate.

"There's nothing there," I wailed.

"Nonsense!" she contradicted. "There are hundreds of openings." She began to reel them off, schools, grades, locations. Some of the names rang bells—alarm bells; the rest were completely alien. On the brink of tears, I interrupted her recitation, deciding to throw myself on her mercy, appeal to her sense of fair play. After all, we were both mature, intelligent women, college-trained professionals. Besides, I figured she "owed me one" for the five minute coffee break I had sanctioned.

"What would *you* suggest?" I pleaded.

She was flattered by my trust. I could tell by the tilt of her head, the twinkle in her eyes, and the delighted smile, that she had been waiting for this moment.

"Well then, how about the Jamison School?" she suggested. "It's the closest to your home, and there's conve-

I wondered if there was anything to be gained by tampering
with the tacks.

nient transportation. The kids are lovely. The principal is a doll. Modern intercom system. Friendly faculty and—" after an almost imperceptible pause as she reviewed my proportions, she concluded "—a fabulous cafeteria." Her pitch was done, and she sat there beaming, waiting for my capitulation.

Oh, Hamlet, I thought. *It isn't only in Denmark that villains smile!*

"Thanks, but no thanks," I answered, unable to completely eliminate the "How could you?" from my voice. "I have already been at the Jamison," I added without elaboration.

Annoyed at being caught, she turned brusque, reminding me that my allotted fifteen minutes were up and that she didn't want to fall behind this early in the day. Pushing a printed form across the desk, she suggested that since I couldn't make up my mind, perhaps I would like to sign a statement refusing assignment for the present.

"If you sign, you will continue as a substitute for the remainder of the semester, and then we'll call you in for another go at the board."

The offer was tempting and safe, but as I picked up the pen to sign the waiver, I remembered my friend Lucille's parting words as she dropped me off that morning on her way to the parking lot.

"If nothing looks good, there's the Knight."

Lucille's son was a physical education teacher at the Knight School, a brand new, two-story, still-to-be-dedicated lower grade center. It *was* inner city, but not as inner as most. "There are a couple of openings in the primary grades," Lucille had vouched. "I'd apply there myself if the rules permitted."

Laying down the pen, I said, "I think I'll take one of the openings at the Knight."

The counselor's eyes widened. "The Knight? Where do you see an opening at the Knight? Did I say anything about the Knight? Look!" She pointed triumphantly at the vacant spot. "See for yourself. No tack!"

I sighed and reached for the pen but then recalled that Lucille, an aggressive soul, would demand an accounting. I could hear her say, "*What?* You took *her* word against *mine?*" Then, too, having lost faith in my counselor, I was also beginning to doubt the infallibility of the tack.

Fully expecting to be shot down a second time, I meekly protested, "But I know someone at the Knight. The gym teacher, Hank Ryan."

In a flash she was out of her chair and across the hall. What had I done? Had she run for reinforcements? Could I be fired for insubordination before I had even been hired? Worse still, had I jeopardized Hank's career?

I heard voices raised in argument from the adjacent office, stepped over to the doorway the better to eavesdrop, and heard my counselor insist, "But she says she knows somebody there!"

There was a sudden cessation of dialogue, and I rushed back to my seat. The murmuring resumed, but less heatedly. Positive that I had stirred up a hornet's nest, I fidgeted anxiously.

A moment later she was back, beaming and waving a sheaf of papers.

"Are you ever in luck!" she gushed. "We have just received notice in this morning's mail that there *is* an opening at the Knight!" To prove it, she pressed a tack into position on the map. "It's a third grade class. Isn't that marvelous?"

I decided I'd better go along with the instant camaraderie, and I agreed that I was indeed most fortunate and it was truly a marvel. Whatever skulduggery was being practiced was not my business, I concluded as I signed the contract for the Knight School.

We shook hands, and we exchanged smiles; but above those smiles our eyes dueled. Hers signaled defensively: "Sorry, but that's the way it is in the System. Now you know."

Mine semaphored: "I'm learning."

"*Clout,*" Everett enlightened me when I arrived home and told him the story. "That's what is known as *clout.*"

I didn't like the sound of the word any more than I had appreciated the unsavory experience of that morn-

ing. I consulted the dictionary, but I could see no con-
nection between what had happened to me at the drop
of a name and the definitions I found in my *American
Collegiate*: "the shot that hits the mark," "cuffing of the
ear."

"Are you sure you know what you're talking about?" I
challenged Everett. After all, a person doesn't pick up
words like that in the Pocono Mountains of Pennsylvania, his point of origin. He quirked a bushy
eyebrow.

I hastened to explain my irreverence. "I mean nobody
ever told me. Not one of my college teachers ever used
the word. None of the students ever bandied it about at
any of our gabfests."

I stored the word away for future analysis. I didn't
have long to wait. Everett was vindicated when a caus-
tic Chicago columnist wrote an essay on "Clout." I
learned that it was a kind of political compatability, like
being on good terms with the precinct captain or having
a cousin at City Hall. In the Chicago school system,
clout was knowing one's way around the 228 Building,
first-naming the consultants in the district office, or, as
in my case, having a friend whose son was a gym teacher on his way to a principalship.

It was inevitable that I should accept the word as a
legitimate one, because I was to become the innocent
beneficiary of the practice more than once. Some of the
most interesting experiences of my teaching career have
happened because I knew someone with influence. For
instance, a friendship that began in a graduate seminar
in Elizabethan literature led to a phone call one June
day, inviting me to work through the summer as an
editor on a special bilingual project.

"But I've had no experience—" I protested, flattered
but apprehensive.

"You *are* a friend of Julie Prescott's, aren't you?" the
voice interrupted impatiently.

"Oh, yes, Julie and I met in Dr. Vincent's seminar—"

"Well, then, report Monday morning at nine in Room
eight forty."

I did as I was directed, and that summer position,

frustrating and fascinating by turns, a chapter out of *Through the Looking Glass*, culminated in a festive dinner at an ethnic restaurant, where I was placed haphazardly at the same table with a language consultant. We hit it off immediately, being of one mind that the summer's project had been an expensive fiasco. We exchanged opinions, anecdotes, and phone numbers, and then we went our respective ways.

"What a lovely person," I told my family. "Too bad I'll never see her again."

Then three days into the fall semester, I was summoned from my high school classroom to participate in a year-long extension of that summer's fiasco—er, project. We were to take the lessons produced during the summer, embellish them with visual aids, and introduce them to classes all over the city. Remembering the quality of the lesson contents, I shuddered. I looked at my principal pleadingly. "Who, me?" I queried. "I have no experience at this sort of thing."

He glanced at the telephone message in his hand. "You *do* know Dr. Young, don't you?"

"Oh, certainly. We shared a bowl of guacamole sauce at the Aztecan Restaurant last August—"

"Well, she wants you to report to her office tomorrow morning to begin a three-week training program."

My husband says I would have been good army material, that I have a "mine but to do or die" mentality. He's probably right. I reported as ordered, and during that year I gave a full measure of devotion under the most harrowing of conditions.

In recognition of my heroic efforts, I was called into the office of an area supervisor at the end of the year. "Do you have a job for this summer?" he asked.

"Not yet," I answered.

"The High School Curriculum Revision Committee needs one more member. Report downtown on Monday," he ordered.

"But I'm only an English teacher," I protested. "I don't know anything about—"

"Just keep your mouth shut for the first couple of weeks. You'll learn."

One day in an American literature class, the kids and I explore the values and the morals of our nation's founders. I make it a point to emphasize the work ethic of our forefathers—the blood, sweat, and tears that lead to success; the early-to-bed, early-to-rise, nose-to-the-grindstone philosophy that promised health, wealth, and wisdom.

"Of course," I begin, intending to purposely provoke the students, "that 'bootstrap' supposition is on the endangered list today, isn't it? Success nowadays depends not on how hard you work, or on how much you know, but on—what?"

"On *who* you know!" several call out.

"*Whom* you know," corrects Clara, the class grammarian.

It is an honors class, and the discussion catches fire spontaneously. There is a vehement denial from Greek-born Areti; a cynical rebuttal from devil's advocate Darren; accusations of "Generalizations—you're making generalizations!" from forensic star Mike. They argue, most of them, on the side of idealism, scorning the clout system, but forced to admit its existence. They have barely begun when the passing bell rings, ending the period. But not the debate. They are still at it as they gather their books and move out into the hall.

"I don't care," Areti reiterates loudly. "It's not *who* you know; it's *what* you know and how hard you work!"

I lock the door behind them, turn off the ceiling lights, take my flattened sandwich out of my attaché case, and retrieve my Coke from the window ledge. The cheese on rye is seven hours old, and the soft drink is tepid. I would fare better in the cafeteria, but I eschew the teachers' lunchroom in favor of a dry morsel and a quiet room.

While I wolf the stale sandwich—was it Emerson or Franklin who maintained that "hunger is the best pickle?"— I reflect on the paradox of clout. My students—and I—would like to believe in an ideal workaday world in which brain, brawn, and integrity—not clout—are the determinants for success. What would their reaction be if I told them that there is another world in which

54

ideally *clout is all*—a perfect realm founded on, of all things, nepotism?

Some of the students, the small percentage who know and share my religious beliefs, would get my drift. Those five or six students who call themselves Christians would recognize the consecrated clout system, in which knowing the *right person* is absolutely vital.

I crumple the wax paper, sweep the crumbs from my lap, and turn my eyes away from the busy bulletin boards and the disordered desks to gaze out the windows and enjoy the vista of sky, clouds, trees, and steeples that are part of the compensation for having to climb to a third-floor classroom. Fifteen minutes into my lunch period in the quiet room, the throbbing stops, my blood pressure drops, and I face a choice: I can correct the ever-mounting pile of papers, or I can meditate and gird my spirits for the next invasion. It isn't a difficult decision; I push aside the papers.

I am intrigued by this new concept of clout; my mind will not leave it alone. Scripture quotations come to mind faster than I can jot them down. "No one comes to the Father *but through Me*" (John 14:6, italics added).

"Neither is there salvation in any other: for there is *none other name* under heaven given among men, whereby we must be saved" (Acts 4:12, KJV*, italics added).

"...that I may know *Him,* and the power of His resurrection..." (Philippians 3:10, italics added).

Praise God, I think, *for sanctified clout!*

Then I descend again in my reverie to the nitty-gritty, the highs and—yes—the lows of my career that result from so-called chance encounters and coincidences that I label "clout," that I attribute to "knowing someone," and I am forced to acknowledge that the word "someone" should be capitalized. Over and above the people who have given me a helping hand has always been God's master plan!

It is five minutes until the bell. I straighten the desks, erase the chalkboard, unlock the door, and take my position in the hall to keep the young people moving, break

* King James Version.

55

up amorous tête-á-têtes, and welcome my next class as they straggle in.

Sandy, always the first to arrive, looks at me long and quizzically and finally says, in a burst of derring-do, "Mrs. Reichel, you look like you enjoyed your lunch!"

"Well, Sandy, I guess I did!"

5
Sammy Jackson

I can grow mold on a dish of tomatoes in the refrigerator and mildew on a pile of dampened clothes destined for the ironing board, but I cannot produce a hardy philodendron or a healthy geranium. African violets recognize me as a killer and shrink from my touch when I enter the florist's shop. My one successful houseplant was a sweet potato vine that garlanded our kitchen; it survived only because I left it strictly alone. Why I ever let my third-graders get me involved in an agricultural experiment is beyond me, unless it was because they kept nagging me with "All the other rooms are doing it, so why can't we?"

I bought a bag of potting soil, and the children saved their milk cartons for planters. It would have been far wiser for me to supply lima beans or a packet of marigold seeds for the project, but I thought they might learn more if each child brought his own seeds: apple, orange, lemon, grapefruit, pumpkin, or whatever.

We set up a gardening table in front of one of the windows, and every day two or three of the children would spend some time planting their seeds, watering them down, labeling their cartons, and then cleaning up the mess. After two weeks of this, everyone had started his crop except Sammy Jackson.

Oh, Sammy had his seeds, all right; he had brought them in on the first day, all safely done up in a rubber-banded aspirin tin. Unfortunately though, I had established a prerequisite: no planting until all the assigned classwork had been finished. Sammy Jackson was a procrastinator of the worst order; every day this incorrigible, but winsome, butterball—four feet tall and almost as wide—would fall farther behind in his work, while he complained—loudly enough for all the class to hear—about the injustice of it all. Finally, weary of his whining, I negotiated a deal with Sammy. I gave him an extra load of "catch up" homework assignments and told him that if he brought them in completed the next day, he would be allowed to plant his seeds.

He brought in his work as requested and handed it to me with a flourish. I thought it best not to ask too many questions.

"Now, kin I plant?"

"Go right ahead, Sammy," I said.

It seemed to me that he took an unreasonably long time at his gardening stint that morning; however, I was busy teaching a social studies lesson, and having Sammy out of the way was a relief.

I don't know how many days we watered, watched, and waited, setting the plants on the sunny windowsills by day, returning them to their draft-free protected corner at night.

"They're not up yet?" the kids would ask each morning. After a few weeks, all but a few of the children had given up, and I am afraid they had lost faith, not only in nature but also in their teacher. Sammy, the last to bury his seeds, still hovered around the table for a few minutes each morning. I watched him closely, knowing somewhat how his mind worked.

One Monday morning I walked into the classroom, raised the blinds, and automatically went to the table where the plants had spent a quiet weekend. I gasped. Every one of those pots had come alive! Each one contained a beautiful, brave little cotyledon! Wordsworth and his host of golden daffodils could not approach the rapture I felt over my twenty-seven seedlings!

When the children straggled into the room and saw the miracle that had transpired over the weekend, there was pandemonium. Roberta, a slip of a girl and an inde-

"They're not up yet?"

pendent thinker, who wore starched pinafores and whose hair was always arranged in a cascade of bouncing black ringlets, was the only one who did not join in the revelry. She sat stiffly at her desk, waiting for me to bring order out of the hugger-mugger. I was so busy doing just that that I figured I could wait until later to find out what was bothering her.

We finally pledged allegiance and sang "My Country, 'Tis of Thee." Then we jumped immediately into an arithmetic lesson. When the papers were collected from that assignment, I directed the children's attention to the new spelling list on the front board.

"Who will volunteer to read these words for the class?"

Roberta's hand shot up.

"All right, Roberta," I nodded, glad she was overcoming her sulk. But reading the spelling words was the farthest thing from Roberta's mind. She had only wanted the floor long enough to challenge me.

"Miz Reichel, how come all dem plants looks de same? How come Stella plants a peach, and I plants a grapefruit, and Mike plants a apple—and dey all looks de same?"

I strolled over to the window to inspect the nursery—and to collect my thoughts. *You got me, Roberta. Are they supposed to look different? Don't all babies look alike? Won't they change as they mature? Now, how am I supposed to know?*

Roberta wasn't finished with me. "And how come, Miz Reichel, dey all come up at de same time—and we planted 'em all at diff'runt times?"

"Yeah." The class was lining up on her side now. There was an accusatory ring to that "Yeah, how come, Miz Reichel?" They were beginning to suspect me of a little hanky-panky at the potting table; a bit of face-saving manipulation over the weekend.

I looked again at those fragile little seedlings. A flash of inspiration struck me. I whirled around.

"Sammy Jackson!" I shouted, pointing my finger at the grinning imp. "When you were up here two weeks ago planting your watermelon seeds, did you tamper with the rest of these cartons?"

The class was holding its collective breath, and every eye was on Sammy. This was the moment for which he had been waiting. He rose to it dramatically. His grin deepened into a beatific smile. His eyes bulged with excitement. Placing his two chubby hands over his ample mid-section, he began to rotate them, proclaiming with gusto:

"Miz Reichel, I sho does *love* watuhmelon!"

6
Philander Bond

I was summoned to the principal's office one overcast morning in January, my ninth month at the Knight School. My palms were sweaty, my stomach churning, and my heart was syncopating. An invitation from the administration always did and always will create havoc within. I don't need to undergo analysis to understand why.

As a child I was a rebel in an authoritarian school system. I can describe to this day the pictures on the wall and the rug on the floor in Sister Frances's office where it all began—where eons ago, a chunky, frightened, but defiant, eight-year-old dared to refuse to take punch cards around from door to door to raise funds for the new convent roof or to repair cracks in the church's foundation. Not that I was a child of high principles, although I believe that was the defense my parents suggested I use. The truth of the matter was that I was more terrified at knocking on strangers' doors and being rejected than I was by this twice a year castigation in the principal's office.

So when I sat across from Mr. Swartz that morning I still carried a lot of residual angst. That's why I perched tentatively on the edge of the leather seat, ready to bolt at the first hint of disapprobation. I had been at the Knight for nine months, and he had yet to visit my classroom to see how I was faring. Never had he given me any indication as to whether or not he was satisfied with my performance. I felt I was doing just fine. And some of the faculty members had given me an encouraging word now and then. Why hadn't *he?*

Ending the telephone conversation that had been in progress when I walked in, he pushed the phone to one side, hunched forward and turned on a most charming smile.

"Sorry I haven't had a chance to chat with you sooner."

"Chat," of course, is a cozy word. Between that and the disarming smile, I decided I could afford to relax, so I settled farther into the chair.

"How do you like it here? Any complaints?"

He didn't wait for an answer. I dare say he knew that anyone coming to the Knight from the Jamison would be abjectly grateful for the rest of her days.

"You know," he confided, "we are so happy to have mature women like yourself entering the profession—"

I stiffened, alerted by the alarm going off somewhere inside my skull. That word "mature" again! So unctiously, so condescendingly tossed into the conversation! That term of inveiglement—where had I heard it before? Ah, yes—the Jamison School. "Women of your maturity," the soon-to-be district supervisor had said, and Lucille and I had lunged for the bait.

I gave Mr. Swartz a reproachful look. He hesitated, and then decided to continue.

"You have a family, don't you, Jocelyn?"

Step Two, I thought; *first name basis. A highly effective ploy when trying to win friends and manipulate teachers, especially effective in my case if the manipulator pronounces my first name correctly.* And Mr. Swartz had.

Grudgingly I offered my four children as evidence. I was in the act of getting out their snapshots when his next remark brought me to a halt.

"That explains the excellent job you're doing in the classroom. Don't think I haven't noticed."

Well, I *did* think so, and why shouldn't I have? But then, after all, he *was* a busy man, with a student body of one thousand, a faculty of forty-five, and a school that was constantly being upset by boundary shifts, gang wars, and midnight vandalism. I wriggled back farther into the chair to hear him out.

He sensed that I had crossed over from cynicism to sympathy, and he struck without further preambling.

"Jocelyn, we have a problem, and I think you can help us."

"Oh?" I murmured politely. It was a professional kind of "Oh?" with a nuance suggesting the interpretation: "You do? You may just have come to the right person. Tell me all about it."

"Miss Wright is having trouble with one of her boys. Philander Bond. There are differences that they can't seem to resolve. It is my opinion that it's no more than a personality conflict."

"Personality conflict," I have since learned, is an educational euphemism for "Listen, Mr. Swartz. It's me or that monster! I refuse to put up with him another day!"

"Miss Wright is quite young and doesn't have the advantage of your experience."

Funny. I never thought of her as being young, I mused. She *was* on the felicitous side of thirty, but compensating for that were her eight or nine years as a teacher—against my eight or nine months.

"Yes," he reiterated, "nothing more than a clash of temperaments. Otherwise I would never make the suggestion—"

"Suggestion?"

"Yes, it's only a suggestion. You may refuse if you wish."

Oh, may I? Indeed? A probationary teacher with one broken contract on her record and almost two and a half years to go until tenure—turn down a suggestion from her principal? Your suggestion is my command, Mr. Swartz!

"I had thought of having Philander transferred to your class. Not immediately. This is Wednesday. Let's say, Monday morning. We'll tell his family we're making the move to level class size, but you and I and Miss Wright will know it's to help Philander."

I went along with the suggestion. First of all, because

I like challenges; and second, because I didn't feel I had a choice in the matter. Not really. That phrase "to help Philander" was also a very effective arm-twister at that point in my career. It took me a few more years in the public school system to learn that very seldom is anything ever done to help Philander—or Juan or Maria. In the Board of Education, as in any bureaucracy, the main priority is job security, and next to that, personal advancement. If, along the way, a child is inadvertently helped, that's fine and dandy, but purely accidental.

I began that same day to look for Philander Bond. Every time Miss Wright took her class anywhere—to the washroom or library, recess or gym—I rushed to my door to give her boys the once-over. Could it be that lumbering, oversized clown with the vacuous grin who took delight in hammer-locking whoever happened to be near him in line? Or was it the frenetic jumping-jack who couldn't pass the water fountain without diverting its stream and soaking his classmates or pushing their faces down into it as they were trying to drink? Or was it—*oh, Lord, please not*—the boy who made barnyard noises all day long—in and out of class, on the playground, and even during fire drill? I could have asked Miss Wright to point out Philander to me, but I didn't want her to know I was anxious. What's more, I really didn't want to know his identity any sooner than necessary.

I told my class we were going to have a new member on Monday, a boy from another room.

"That's all we needs, is anothuh boy!" Roberta was disgusted.

"He can't have *my* desk," threatened Tiger Marshfield, his freckled face squeezed into an ugly mask, and his skinny pale arms and legs wrapped as far around his portable desk as he could manage.

"I hope he don't like it here and goes back where he come from," said Jennie Lou Scarbeary, my tow-headed tomboy from Tennessee. "We'uns is just perfect the way we is!"

Those were my sentiments, too, and I felt like giving her a great big hug, but I rallied and returned to reality.

"Isn't anyone thinking about the new boy's feelings?

65

Put yourself in his place. How would you like moving to a new classroom in the middle of the year, having to get used to a different teacher? Leaving all your old friends behind you and having to make all new ones?" I let them empathize for a few moments, and then I said, "We've got to make him feel at home. Who's got some ideas?"

Sammy Jackson was the quickest to respond. Grinning happily and half-falling out of his seat in his excitement, he yelled, "Yes, ma'am! I kin fights wid him!"

Sammy had the disconcerting habit of precipitating wrestling matches at the drop of a pencil—or just from sheer boredom. The class would be industriously doing their spelling or whatever; I would be busy tutoring a student at my desk—and then, out of the blue would come the thud of falling bodies, the scuffling and scratching of cleated boots, and the grunts and pantings of an impromptu set-to. I'd rush to the scene and start to pull apart the combatants, only to find both of them grinning up at me, and Sammy insisting, "We wuz only playin', Miz Reichel. Honest!"

"If you start a fight with this new boy, I'll give you a week's detention!" I promised.

"I kin show him around the room 'n tell him where everything is, ekcetera, ekcetera," offered Tiger Marshfield, his grip on his desk relaxed and his demoniac leer replaced by an innocent, wide-eyed, and ingratiating smile.

"You do that, Tiger, and you will forfeit recess and gym for a week!" Tiger was well aware he was allowed to leave his seat only with my permission. In our small class, eighteen children since the latest redistricting, I had permitted the children to work at special projects located around the room. They were free to go to these areas when their assigned lessons were completed. At first Tiger had enjoyed this privilege along with the rest of the class until we found he was the one who had emptied the mouse's water and food containers just before 3:00 each day, hidden the key pieces to our expensive educational jigsaw puzzles, and surreptitiously removed—a few at a time—the tiny plastic clips from our new vertical blinds, making them inoperable.

I put the problem of Philander on hold over the weekend. When I signed in Monday morning, I was rested and confident that I would find a solution to whatever problems Philander would bring with him (unless he was, indeed, the barnyard ventriloquist!). I ran into Miss Wright at the mailboxes.

"I'll send Philander over after I take attendance," she said curtly.

I didn't like the idea of Philander dropping in on his own, even though he had only a twenty-foot corridor to cross. It might occur to him that he had to make a grand entrance. I couldn't risk that.

"I'll come to get him, if you don't mind," I said, pitting my ten-year chronological advantage against her eight years of experience.

"Suit yourself," she answered.

After our opening exercises and roll call, I told the sleepy-eyed youngsters I was going to fetch our new member. I warned them that I wanted a quiet reception, even if they happened to recognize the boy. No hooting. No hollering. They were to sit politely and wait for me to make the introductions. They nodded their heads apathetically. Because Sunday evening church services kept most of them up until after midnight, there were seldom any discipline problems on Monday morning.

I crossed the hall to Miss Wright's room. Barely acknowledging my presence, she called out contemptuously, "Philander! Get your things. Mrs. Reichel is here to escort you to her room!"

I hid my annoyance—and my anxiety—as I waited to find out which of the boys was Philander. In the last seat and in the last row, as far away from Miss Wright's desk as she could place him, a small boy was trying to gather together his possessions: outdoor clothing—a formidable armful since this was January—along with a schoolbag, gym paraphernalia, some loose pens and pencils, and a handful of rulers and paintbrushes. He would never make it in one trip, especially with all our eyes on him, but he was valiantly trying. He was just a little

67

tyke; his defenselessness caught me like a physical blow. I wanted to get him out of there as quickly as possible, so I reached for the nearest boy, half-pulled him from his seat, and sent him to rescue Philander.

After helping Philander stow his belongings in his new hall locker, I dismissed the reluctant recruit, led my new charge over to the empty hall-guard chair outside the door of my room, and sat down. I took Philander's hands in mine and with our eyes on a level I was able to look him full in the face for the first time. He was a handsome boy; his face was a perfect oval of rich mahogany, crowned by a close cap of tight black curls. I looked for signs of mischief, guile, or evasiveness. There were none. His eyes were brimming over with love; he tried, but he couldn't suppress the wide, beatific smile and the happiness spilling over.

I had forgotten just what it was I had been going to say to Philander—something about "Here's your chance to make a new start—I just know you and I are going to hit it off—" No matter. I noticed in our comfortable silence that his clothes were obviously brand-new: stiff corduroy slacks, sharp turtlenecked shirt in multi-colored stripes. It was a message to me from his mother: This is my boy, whom I love very much. I want you to love him, too.

He had a gold pin on the front of his shirt, so small I almost missed it. Three letters welded together into the word *joy*. I had seen that pin before, and I felt safe asking him what the letters stood for.

"Do you know, Philander?" I asked.

"Yes'm."

"Tell me, Philander."

"Jesus first, Others second, Ourselves last—and that spells 'joy'!"

I was soon to discover that he wore that pin every day.

"Then you're a Christian?" I asked.

"Yes'm."

"So am I."

"Yes'm."

Well, what did I expect a shy, nine-year-old to say? "Praise the Lord"?

"That's going to make things easier for you and me," I told him.

He agreed.

"Whenever you have a problem, you can come to me, and we can pray about it together. How about that?"

That, too, was evidently fine with Philander. I resisted the impulse to hug him and took him into the room to introduce him to his new classmates, who behaved quite admirably. Philander was too small, too friendly, and too eager to please to constitute a threat to the comfortable community that was our classroom. As a matter of fact, before the week had gone by, Philander had become the class darling. The children fought for the privilege of being his partner in line, helping him with his arithmetic, and coaching him in spelling. Roberta's assertiveness led her to become Philander's defender—even against me.

"Miz Reichel, you givin' Philander too much homework all at once. You oughta work him up to it gradual, like."

Tiger announced to the class at large one day that it was all right for Philander to touch his desk. "Philander, understand! No one else!" And Sammy Jackson reassured me that I wouldn't have to worry about his wrestling Philander, " 'Cuz ah already done it, at recess, and all he done was jist roll up in a ball and laff his head off!"

As for the relationship between Philander and me, I don't think we ever fell out of love. Philander brought me his Sunday school papers each Monday morning. On Valentine's Day he came to school early with a three-pound box of chocolates—a beribboned, cupid-decorated heart bought with his own money from the local drugstore. I asked him to let me share it with the class—and he gladly consented. That afternoon as I read from Meindert de Jong's *Wheel on the School*, Philander proudly passed the candy around twice—once for each chapter.

Oh, it could have been a far more dramatic story if

On Valentine's Day he came to school early with a three-pound box of chocolates ... bought with his own money from the local drugstore.

Philander had turned out to be the overgrown bully in Miss Wright's class who tormented everyone within reach. Or if there had been a child prodigy behind that angelic smile and compliant personality, a genius waiting to be awakened by an inspiring teacher. But why conjecture? I loved Philander the way he was; and the way he was—even working to his full capacity—was average. Whatever problems he'd had in Miss Wright's room—interesting or not—he left them there. Philander never caused me a moment's concern, except perhaps that I worried because of that very fact—that he was always on his good behavior.

"I know what you mean," his mother told me over the phone, "but Philander isn't 'on his good behavior.' Philander just doesn't have any really bad behavior. The only behavior he's got is good! How I wish I could say that about my five other children!"

Philander spelled *love* in our classroom. Perhaps the children instinctively sensed my special feeling for Philander. Perhaps it had nothing to do with me at all, but only that they too felt his goodness. Roberta shed her aggressive cynicism—had she noticed that it distressed Philander when she challenged my authority? Sammy Jackson considered Philander his only true friend—was it because he was the only one who did not taunt Sammy because of his size? And there were no more wrestling bouts.

The last week of school, when we had to find a home for Henry, our white mouse, Tiger Marshfield suggested Philander take him, because he would treat him better than anyone else. And all the class agreed.

7
Andrew

It's chill November, and the communiqué from the office reminds us to keep our classroom doors closed and to pull down the window shades each afternoon before we leave the building. The windows of my room face north, and the heating system in this sixty-year-old wing of the high school complex is undependable. There is no need to prod me into compliance. I lower the shades to the sills and keep the doors locked against the arctic blasts that barrel down the hallways. I also add a few survival touches of my own, like English snuggies, a handy Thermos of hot soup, and pile-lined boots. Then I position myself near the lukewarm radiators while I teach.

It's dreary November, and at 6:45 the mornings are dark—and my room is darker. Groping for the light switch, I think of Andrew. I will never be able to enter a darkened classroom *without* thinking of him.

I met Andrew in my second year of teaching. It was my second assignment—a small, neighborhood elementary school on an elm-shaded street within walking distance of home—a plum of an assignment after a year and a half in the inner city. Arriving eager and early on my first day, I was introduced to the school clerk, then to the principal, and lastly to Andrew. (That particular order—clerk, principal, custodian—may have been accidental; I prefer to think it was a presage of proper protocol.)

He was waiting for me in my second-floor classroom. "I am Andrew Barr, the custodian," the stocky, stern-faced, white-thatched gentleman informed me. The word *custodian* took on dignity as he pronounced it. I was not exactly sure what a custodian in the Chicago public schools did. I'd had experience with engineers, janitors, matrons, and window washers, but never with anyone who called himself a "custodian." I surveyed the nattily-attired man, who looked as though he were bound for a day on the links—Saint Andrews, judging from his speech. His Caledonian burr was right out of Bobby Burns.

Here is a man, I thought, *whose heart's in the Highlands.* I warmed to him on the spot.

"You're a Scotsman!" I gushed, extending my hand. "Well, *I'm English,*" I offered, expecting to establish a common bond.

His dour expression only deepened. "I'll try to overlook it," he promised unsmilingly, and before I could recover from the put-down, he proceeded with my orientation. Although I was still reeling, I managed to get his message *in toto.* He advised me that he was in charge of the physical appearance of the building, but that he was not paid to pick up after sloppy children and lazy teachers; nor would he condescend to do so. Furthermore, if I expected him to dust the chalkboard troughs, I must see to it that the erasers and the chalk were placed thus and so. As to the wastebaskets, the smaller ones were to be emptied into the larger, and the larger was to be placed to the right of the door each afternoon before I left the building. Finally, the top of my desk was to be cleared of all clutter, or there would be no dusting.

"And one more thing," he warned in conclusion, his eyes narrowing into crescents. "Ye look to me like the kind of teacher that keeps sweets in your desk drawers. We want no rats or roaches around here."

What? I thought. *No "wee, slikit, cow'rin', tim'rous Beasties"?* But I held my peace. It was neither the time nor the place to defend my practice of keeping a bag of caramels in my drawer in the event that one of my diabetic pupils was to suffer from an attack of hypoglycemia. That had not happened as yet, and it was just as well, for I had forgotten the symptoms, anyway, but in the meantime the caramels had been a handy reward for good conduct and excellent performance—the children's as well as mine.

"I would say he was a wee bit o'erpowerin', " I told Everett that night as I described my first encounter with Andrew. "I figure he must be descended from one of those Scots 'wha hae wi' Wallace bled,' and I'm afraid he'll never forgive my being English."

"You're only half-English," my husband reminded me. "Maybe you can work out a compromise."

However, my first, intuitive impression appeared to be prophetic. "Lay the proud usurpers low!" Robert Bruce had commanded, and across the centuries Andrew heard and obeyed. His modus operandi was intimidation, and I was to be its vulnerable victim for five years.

I said Andrew referred to himself as a "custodian." It was not long before I discovered the full meaning of the word. A custodian, as Andrew interpreted the role, was a landscape artist, a janitor, a father-confessor, a Dutch uncle, and a prime mover. Engineers and principals tend to come and go; after all, they are on their way up to larger schools and higher salaries. Clerks are barricaded behind counters where they are confined to payroll paperwork, attendance shenanigans, keeping the principal out of trouble with the district superintendent, and keeping the teachers out of trouble with the principal. But the custodian is the very cement of the school. Not only was Andrew well aware of the vital nature of his position, he intended to educate me as quickly as possible.

I found I was under Andrew's surveillance most of the day. "Stalks me like a deer," I told Everett.

Even during outdoor recess, when one might expect to find the custodial staff on a coffee break, Andrew puttered around in the fenced-off garden that was his particular pride and joy. He was not there to coddle his goldenrod and asters. He was there to field errant balls and to fend off their would-be retrievers; also to take potshots at teachers on duty who did not keep their charges in line.

I must point out in my own defense that, given four solid walls, stationary desks, and enough textbooks to go around, I can maintain discipline with the best of teachers; but surround me with two hundred boys on a half-acre of playground, and my efficiency rating plummets. In such a situation I tend to take cover in a sheltered doorway or behind a tree and pray that the casualties will be light.

Andrew, insensitive to my playground problem, delighted in flushing me out. About the time that the pandemonium and mayhem reached the danger point—two minutes before the bell—Andrew would set aside his trowel or rake and lean on the fence, watching my predicament with withering scorn. His right eyebrow would twitch and shoot up an inch or so, the corners of his mouth would turn down in disgust, and as clearly as if he had enunciated the words, I would hear the message, "What's the matter, woman? Dinna ye ken how to handle the lads?"

My conditioned-response to the stimulus of Andrew's elevated eyebrow was soon firmly established. He had only to glance casually in my direction, and I would lash out at Ricky or Robert or Ramon or whoever was within lashing distance, passing on the intimidation like a hot potato. I admit, reluctantly, that the system worked, for while I dealt with the closest offender, the other 199 boys would cease their fisticuffs and maulings to see who was "getting it" this time, how much, and for what reason.

There were other special occasions that required Andrew's supervision, like the monthly assembly programs. Andrew never missed an assembly. Indeed, he dressed for the occasion, donning a bow tie that he kept in his locker. And when the performance was over, he would drop into my room with his evaluation.

"If I may have a minute, please—" he would ask, and then, peremptorily take over the class. Nothing ever escaped his notice. He had suggestions to make about the precision, or lack of it, with which we marched to and from the stage; he cited the failure of certain students—and he named names—to stand quietly in place; he chided me for the insecure altos who flatted on the last verse; he praised the sopranos who "warbled like nightingales." The compliments he directed to the children; the brickbats he tossed in my general direction. It was evident to me that if anything went right in these musical performances, it was the native talent of the pupils; and whatever went wrong was the fault of the poorly-trained and ill-equipped teacher.

Nevertheless, it was impossible to deny him the opportunity, for the children looked forward to his post-assembly visits like actors waiting up for the early edition. We could not resume the academic grind until Andrew's review was in.

"They are more interested in *his* approval than in *mine*," I complained petulantly to Mavis, the eighth grade teacher across the hall. But then, who was I to murmur? I realized one day that I was no better than my pupils, for I was putting together a medley of Scottish songs for the upcoming assembly, and I was more concerned about Andrew's approbation than that of the music supervisor who was to be our special guest. We spent an inordinate amount of time rehearsing, stealing from math and social studies to do so. It seemed well worth the effort; the children had never sung so well or so enthusiastically. Or so I thought.

Then one afternoon in the middle of a particularly energetic practice session, Andrew stormed into the room, brandishing his dustpan like a claymore! Methought I heard the skirling of bagpipes in the background!

"What in the worrrld are ye doin' to 'Annie Laurie'?" he demanded. Not waiting for a reply, he bade me sit "doon," ordered the "lads" and "lassies" to sit "oop," and then, propping his broom and dustpan in the corner, he proceeded to sing the song in the style of Henry Lauder and like the proper love ballad that it was. He slurred, he trilled, he sustained, he paused here and there for dramatic effect, and at the end he let the words "I'll lay me doon and dee" fade away in a passionate whisper.

Well, all right, so we had been guilty of desecration. While the children applauded exuberantly and Andrew grandly wiped away his tears and blew his nose, I dredged up a comment that would mollify him and save face—mine.

"There is no way, Andrew," I shook my head regretfully, "that we can come anywhere near a performance like that. One has to be born a Scot and a singer both. But we'll do the best we can," I promised.

There was no hiding from Andrew. Not even during the lunch hour. He made it his business to be present daily in the children's lunchroom, a basement area set aside for the convenience of forty or so "latchkey" pupils. We teachers were assigned a two-week lunchroom stint each semester. To most of us it was the most odious of fringe duties, and I for one officiated with dispatch. There was a close and secret competition between Mavis and me to see who could clear the lunchroom in the shortest time. She dubbed my reign "The Fortnighter's Bolt and Run Diner"; I retaliated with "Mavis's Galloping Gourmet Cafe." I was never able to match her record: in at 12:00 and out at 12:10. The closest I ever got was 12:12, and that on a sunny day when the ice cream truck played its seductive melody outside the windows.

Andrew hovered over these peanut butter and jelly sessions for only one reason. He was not concerned with how long it took me to clear the area, but how *well* I cleared it. He stood ready with a damp cloth so that I could wipe the tables after the mass exodus, and if I missed a crumb or two in my haste to get to my own lunch, he would call attention to my oversight with an accusing finger. I accepted the K.P. duty with as much grace as possible, taking comfort from the assumption that all of us teachers were in this together. It was not until five years had passed, on the day of my farewell luncheon, that I found out differently. My self-esteem slipped the last few notches when Andrew complimented me with the encomium: "I'll miss ye. You're the only teacher in the whole school to wipe the tables in the kiddies' lunchroom!"

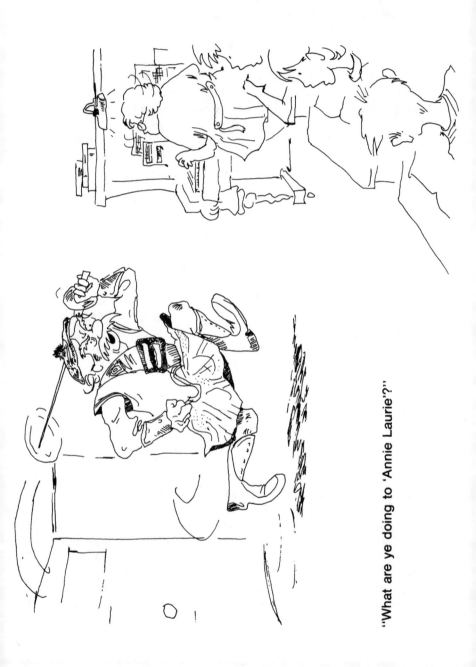

"What are ye doing to 'Annie Laurie'?"

"It could have been worse," Everett comforted. "He could have been standing by with a wet mop."

Andrew became my own special problem, I suppose, because I am a listener by nature. "Spell that 'pushover,'" said Mavis, when I went to her one day with a tale of woe, hoping she could come up with a solution. Andrew had begun to take over my preparation hour, the time from 7:45 to 8:45, the quiet time when I braced myself physically and spiritually for the day's grind. At first, his visits had been brief, but eventually he was monopolizing all my free time, dropping in to reminisce, advise, and philosophize. Having been reasonably well brought up, I tried to show respect to my elders. I was also easily cowed. So whenever I saw Andrew approaching, I automatically assumed a polite and interested posture, made appropriate and commiserating responses, cultivated the virtue of long-suffering, and went home and took it out on my husband.

"Lock him out," Everett said. "You have a key, don't you?"

Well, of course. Why hadn't I thought of that myself? The next morning I acted on Everett's advice, locked the door, and moved my work to the back of the room where I couldn't be seen from the hall. I settled in happily, but not for long. Andrew was not deterred. Finding his way barred, he got out his master key, unlocked the door, and entered, laughing at my "security measures."

"Did you ever think of telling him you're too busy to socialize?" Everett asked.

I agreed to try the candid approach, but only because I was frantically trying to prepare a special exhibit for a district meeting.

"Oh, Andrew," I moaned when he dropped in the following morning. "I just don't have time to visit. I've got so much to do—"

My plea failed. To Andrew it was a cue, not a discouragement.

"Busy!" he snorted. "You think *you're* busy! Wait till ye hear what I've got to do! His list was long and his descriptions elaborate; when the children rushed into the cloakroom forty-five minutes later, he was still going strong.

Mavis could not understand my dilemma. She had effectively alienated Andrew years ago—sized him up within five seconds of their introduction and took the offensive by having him transport all her music and art supplies from her station wagon to the third floor. After that initial intimidation, whenever she saw him on the horizon, she would have another onerous task on the tip of her tongue. Consequently, he was careful to keep out of her range.

Although unable to sympathize with me, Mavis did make a rescue attempt. She bought me a sign; a no-monkey-business, done-with-pussyfooting DO NOT DISTURB cardboard placard. She ordered me to tape it to my classroom door.

In her own way, Mavis could be as formidable as Andrew. I figured I was doomed either to founder on Scylla or drown in Charybdis, so I had nothing to lose. I affixed the sign to the door the next day and tried to appear feverishly at work—not too difficult, since I was grading report cards. I heard Andrew approach, his heavy work shoes loud in the deserted hallway. I sensed his shock and indignation as he read the sign. I fought hard against the temptation to glance up and smile and say, "Oh, come on in, Andrew. It's only a joke!"

The sad sound of his retreating footsteps tormented me the rest of the day—and for weeks afterward. I had lost a confidante of sorts—and a janitor. My blackboards went unwashed, layers of dust accumulated, wastebaskets were emptied only when filled to overflowing. Of more concern to me than the housekeeping, however, was the damaged relationship.

"Don't worry about it," Mavis argued. "You're rid of the old nuisance. Besides, it's only temporary. He'll come around. He'll have to—you're the only audience he has."

She was right. He returned on a November morning. I walked into my darkened classroom, and before I could reach for the light switch, I heard him. He was crying. I changed my mind about the light. My eyes adjusted to the dim surroundings, and I saw him huddled at my desk, his head cradled in his arms, his shoulders heaving. My initial reaction was not admirable. I resented his usurping my desk. I was vexed at the thought that here was a situation that was going to drain me of what little vitality I possessed so early in the day. And I was afraid—afraid of whatever it was that could make this grown man weep.

I sank into a student desk near him. "What's wrong, Andrew?" I asked, reluctantly unstopping the bottle. *Was it his wife,* I wondered. *One of his sons? A grandchild?*

At the sound of my voice, he slowly—and grandly— lifted his head and blew his nose noisily on the handkerchief that had been balled up in his fist, in an obviously valiant attempt to regain his composure. I bided my time with eyes averted. Just because he had a sense of the dramatic did not mean he was insincere, I reminded my cynical self.

"Oh, my," he sighed heavily. "I've had such a ghastly life! You've nae idea how miserrrable it's been. Ye must listen to me!"

A wave of *dejà vu* engulfed me. *Where? When?* And then I remembered, and I almost whispered, "Unhand me, grey beard loon!" Not that he had touched me, but like Coleridge's wedding guest, I was impaled by a glittering eye. I slumped back in my seat. I knew I "could not choose but hear." There would be no denying Andrew's urgency.

He began with his unhappy childhood in an Edinburgh slum; his teens spent working in the mines near Fife, sometimes in salt water up to his waist; the steerage trip to the States with his wife, a frail lassie who almost died en route; and then the scrabbling to make a living, until finally, when he was nearly forty, the security of his present job. None of his story was new to me; I had been listening to Andrew for almost five years. Listening and marveling at the determination that had lifted him from the tenement to where he has now, a year and a half from retirement on a very adequate pension, a lovely mortgage-free home, a happy life, and children and grandchildren galore.

That should be enough material success for any man, I thought. *No cause for tears.*

But I had misjudged Andrew. Between sobs he told me that what he had now was only second-best; that he had a dream that would never be fulfilled, and the disappointment was more than he could bear.

Forced to drop out of school at the age of eleven, he had promised himself he would work and save and return to complete his education. He was determined to become a dominie (teacher), to sit on a platform at his own desk—he pounded mine in frustration—and to be a man respected in the community by young and old alike; not to be just a janitor. The word *janitor* was difficult for him to pronounce—he had never before referred to himself as anything but "custodian."

He wept over the opportunity that had never knocked, the bills and responsibilities that had clipped his wings. Bitterly and graphically he emphasized the irony of his life—that the closest he had come to teaching was sweeping classroom floors, policing the washrooms, and spreading sawdust over the vomit of sick children.

I attempted to interrupt, to point out his positive influence. The affection the children had for him. The spotless halls. The award-winning garden. He would not be comforted. Like the Ancient Mariner, he seemed to say, until "my ghastly tale is told, this heart within me burns."

The 8:45 bell rang, and Andrew left before the children could see his ravaged face. I walked to the door and waited to greet the boys and girls, and in the few seconds I had to myself, I tried to shake off the pall left by Andrew's confession.

It is fifteen years since I left Andrew's school. Andrew is gone now. Dead. And Mavis, too. The majestic elms that shaded my windows are gone, also—victims of the beetle and the axe.

Everett, reading over my shoulder, adds, "And you and I, darling, are not long for this world, either!" Well,

I suppose if one has a tendency to slop over, as I do, it is good to have a down-to-earth companion who will curb one's sentimentality from time to time. Someone to shake the oatbag and remind one there's work to be done, today to be lived.

But I keep remembering Andrew, especially in the winter when I walk into the darkened classroom and half expect to find him at my desk. And as long as I remember him I will never be able to rid myself of the feeling—true or not—that I share part of the responsibility for his unhappiness—that often during our five-year acquaintance I did not press hard enough in our conversations about Christ. I was so busy proving to him that I was an effective teacher that I failed to impress him as an effective Christian.

I was, in fact, the very antithesis of 1 Corinthians 13:4-5: "Love is kind, gentle, benign, pervading and penetrating the whole nature, mellowing all that would have been harsh and austere. . .does not brag, nor does it show itself off. . .does not have an inflated ego. . .*is not irritated, provoked, exasperated, aroused to anger.* . . ."*

Oh, Andrew, if you could only come back, we'd rerun that last scene, and this time we'd cry together over the spilled milk of missed chances and fumbled opportunities!

* Kenneth S. Wuest, *The New Testament: An Expanded Translation* (Grand Rapids: Eerdmans, 1961).

8
Words Aptly Spoken

I have always admired articulate people, especially those who can think on their feet and who seem to have an unending supply of *bons mots* to fit the situation—or to save it. I have known many teachers who had the gift, and even a few pupils. Robert Redstone was one of the latter.

Robert entered my fourth grade class late in the fall, having moved into the neighborhood from downstate Illinois. He was a handsome, apple-cheeked boy with smiling eyes—outgoing, personable, fun-loving, and quick-witted. I gave him a partner to see him through the complexities of his first day, but it proved unnecessary. By 3:15 Bob had made himself at home and had a coterie of friends hanging on his every word. At the end of the day he stopped at my desk long enough to declare, "I like it here! It's a neat school. The kids are swell, and so are you!"

Robert could easily have been an A student, but he was satisfied with B's. I had the impression he thought A's might make him a little less popular with the rest of the boys, and for that reason they weren't worth the effort. He was irrepressible at times, especially in speaking out, but his remarks were never cruel or cutting. They were refreshingly unique. More than once he came to our rescue with words to fit the occasion. My favorite recollection involves the science fair that I bravely encouraged my fourth graders to put together.

Chemistry and physics had been my poorest subjects in high school and college, and I had no business pushing my luck by sponsoring a science fair, but our new principal had been a science teacher and was interested in promoting scientific activities in the curriculum.

The children responded enthusiastically when I suggested the fair, and I decided the safest thing I could do was to rely heavily on the Mr. Wizard books, which were popular in the middle grades and whose material was safely within my grasp. Those pupils who were blessed with ambitious parents produced some fascinating projects; the rest of the class went along with me and Mr. Wizard and grew molds, created magnet games, and proved that air has weight—all the mediocre "experiments" that originate in a classroom where the teacher's true love is literature.

For the kids it was a real "happening"; they had spent weeks in preparation, and the excitement mounted as the day approached. Each pupil had constructed a full-sized poster to dramatize his exhibit, and these colorful ads were hung on the walls around three sides of the room. Tables covered with paraphernalia also lined the perimeters, and each child planned to stand between poster and table ready to explain in a carefully rehearsed paragraph or two what his demonstration was all about. Other classes had been invited to visit the fair in the afternoon, but the principal (whom I shall call Mr. Novak) wanted an appearance at 11:30. It was the children's own suggestion to remain in the room at recess and have a dry-run in preparation for Mr. Novak's arrival.

Robert was the unanimous choice for host, and he dressed appropriately: perky bow tie, sparkling white shirt, two-piece suit. I hadn't rehearsed him, having discovered he was much better in a spontaneous situation. When the principal arrived, Bob graciously welcomed him, escorting him to the first table where two pretty young girls had readied an attractive display on capillary action. Stalks of celery were immersed in glasses of colored water, and the girls were more thrilled than anyone else about what they had accomplished.

They could hardly wait to share their information with the principal, but before either of them could begin the presentation, Mr. Novak took charge.

"Aha!" he exclaimed. "Osmosis!" And then he went on to explain the entire process, never noticing the crestfallen, despairing looks of the exhibitors or Bob's helpless shrug of the shoulders and significant glances in my direction. I did make an attempt; I caught Mr. Novak's eye and waved my arms helplessly in the direction of the children and managed to get out one ineffectual "Mr. Novak?" in an effort to alert him to the situation, but he misread me.

"Better move along, eh? Not too much time. Don't want to neglect any of these youngsters and their fine work, do we? What's this next one? Oh, yes, don't tell me—the advantages of streamlining!"

Down the line and around the room he went, picking up the objects so carefully gathered and prepared by the children, using them to explain to the class what they already knew and had wanted to impart to *him*. There was no holding him back.

I can't remember now, so many years later, why I was unable to call a halt to his one-man show. He deserved, certainly, to be stopped. Perhaps it was the incredibility of the experience. *It just could not be happening,* I thought; *no one could possibly be so obtuse!* Or maybe it was the realization that the children would be able to bounce back from this disappointment much more readily than Mr. Novak would be able to recover from the humiliation of being muzzled. At any rate, I held my peace while he displayed his erudition from project to project. Then, after a few final words he was ready to leave, and Robert Redstone, straight-faced, thanked him for coming and escorted him out into the hall.

I took a deep breath. What could I say to the children that wouldn't be disrespectful to the principal and yet would heal their wounded egos? Nine-year-old Robert saved the day. Closing the door and making sure Mr. Novak was out of earshot, Robert, in his piping, penetrating voice, barely able to suppress a giggle, declared:

"He sure stole our thunder, didn't he, Mrs. Reichel?"

Whatever dismay or resentment or frustration had been building up during the principal's monologue was washed away in the tumult of laughter triggered by Bob's comment. Even those who had never heard the expression before caught on, and for weeks after, "stealing our thunder," or variations thereupon, became a byword in our classroom. I finally put a weak-hearted stop to it when I heard the kids refer to the principal as "Chief Thunder Stealer."

Three years later, when I was teaching seventh and eighth grades in the same school, I had many of the same children in my room, including Robert. It was Robert and his quick wit that again saved the day when Mr. Novak dropped into our honors reading class where we were enjoying *The Adventures of Tom Sawyer*. On that particular day, we were discussing the humor of Samuel Clemens and deciding just what it was that made us laugh out loud as we read.

Mr. Novak sat through about ten minutes of the period and then asked if he could say a few words. I thought surely he was going to commend the lively class on its participation and perception. How wrong I was! Instead, he committed the unpardonable sin of criticizing a teacher before her class, compounding the transgression by insulting the intelligence of the pupils.

"You know," he said, addressing the class as well as me, "this book is completely inappropriate for you children. You can't be expected to understand the river town society, the Southern dialect or the black dialect. The humor is even too much for you to handle. After all, it was written over a hundred years ago. In my opinion," and here he turned to me, "you've made a very poor choice."

I didn't answer. I would have had to aim my remarks at the back of his head in order to do so, because he made a hurried exit. Even if he had given me an opportunity to defend myself—and *Tom Sawyer*—I don't think I could have done so. It would have been, according to my traditional training, highly unethical to argue with the principal in front of the children. So I did something that was only *somewhat* unethical.

Taking advantage of the shocked silence, I held my peace for a moment longer until I thought my voice was under control, and then I said, with a touch of playful irony, "Well, it looks as though Mr. Novak thinks *Tom Sawyer* is a bit beyond your comprehension."

I had intended to add, "What do *you* think?" But before I could continue, Robert spoke out, and with perfect timing and just enough good-natured, low-keyed emphasis, he put the whole incident into proper perspective.

"Aw, what does *he* know? He's only a principal!" The class wildly applauded his observation, and I abandoned the rest of my ethics and let them. Finally we returned to Tom and Becky and Huck and Injun Joe and all those other complex characters "beyond their comprehension," who reappeared with added gusto.

Thank you, Robert, wherever you are, for your "words so aptly spoken!"

The right words can change the climate in a classroom. One quotation that I began to use as a safety valve for me and an emotional release for the students is the line from Gray's "Elegy in a Country Churchyard" that reads: "Full many a flower is born to blush unseen,/And waste its sweetness on the desert air." I picked it up from Maude Groom, my English teacher at Northern Baptist Seminary. Whenever Mrs. Groom found our class failing repeatedly to respond to her questioning, she would exclaim with no small measure of exasperation: "Am I wasting my sweetness on the desert air?" That quote relieved both her tension and ours, made us less afraid of responding, and all in all, saved the situation.

According to the writer of Proverbs, the right words at the right time are like "apples of gold in settings of silver" (25:11). Those who bring liberating words are "like the cold of snow in the time of harvest" (25:13).

When I went out to teach, I had a goodly number of apt expressions on file, in the back of my mind and on the top of my head—aphorisms that would entertain and stimulate. But occasionally situations called for more than a line of poetry or an adage from Ben Franklin—

crisis times when I was backed into a corner and had to pray for the right words. Then the Lord responded with the perfect combination, the "apples of gold" that delivered me.

I had been teaching for a year and a half at the fourth grade level. There was going to be an opening in the eighth grade in January. I applied for it and was accepted. For several months prior to the semester changeover, the young substitute in charge of that class was having an extremely difficult time. I knew firsthand, because my room was directly below his, and despite the heavy construction of the old building, I could hear the yelling, the running and stomping, the crashing of overturned desks and who-knew-what-else, all day and every day. The kindest thing I can say for that substitute is that he hung in there for so long.

The class that I was to inherit had been an exemplary one before the substitute had taken over, and I knew they could be again, but I was concerned, nevertheless. The substitute had let it slip that he was leaving and that the fourth-grade teacher would be taking over for the rest of the year. He was supposed to have kept this a secret but had pulled it out as a retaliatory weapon one day when the kids had been particularly obstreperous. They were furious at the news, and as the day of their "indignity" approached, their anger mounted. A fourth-grade teacher is all right to talk to on the playground and in the lunchroom, but what does she know about teaching eighth grade?

The rumbling increased, and teachers around me shook their heads in concern. I was still on probation; two months to go until tenure. It was clear that they doubted my ability to handle such an incendiary situation, and their skepticism began to undermine my own confidence.

On "moving day" a bell rang at 11:00 in the morning, and the teachers who were going to change left their classes and traveled to their new rooms. I picked up my briefcase and shopping bag and said a final farewell to my youngsters, who had never looked so good. Any sadness they might have felt was alleviated by the knowledge that for one day they were going to have the popular substitute who had made things so jolly for the kids upstairs!

I met him at the halfway point on the landing. He looked a mess, hassled and harried, as though he were being pursued. Hardly pausing in his flight, he shouted at me, "You'd better get up there in a hurry! They're madder than blazes! They'll tear the place apart!"

I went on to the top of the stairs. I could hear the sounds of bedlam all right. His warning hadn't been necessary. Well, the kids would have to wait. I needed a few seconds to pray. I set my bag down at the top of the stairs and tuned out as best I could the cacaphony a few feet away. "Dear Lord, give me quietness and confidence. And please, Lord, the right words—"

I didn't know what He would have me say, if anything, but after I finished praying I walked unafraid into that den of lions.

Most of the kids were out of their seats, shouting, throwing books back and forth across the room, shooting spitballs toward the ceiling, and dancing to a radio blaring away on the windowsill. I closed the door behind me, walked over to my desk, set down the armful of materials I had been carrying, balanced the shopping bag and briefcase against my deskdrawers, and then stood there in the classical teacher position, arms folded, my face as impassive as I could make it. I stood there calmly, surveying the wild scene, confident that the teenagers' curiosity would settle them down faster than anything I could do.

Someone thought to turn off the radio; the yelling stopped, and eventually even the whispers, and they began to drift back to their seats. When it was absolutely still, I said in words I had not prepared or even known I was going to say—but which I'm sure were an answer to my stairtop prayer:

"To think I had to wait a year and a half—for *this!*" I looked reproachfully at them and at the shambles their room had become.

"To think I had to spend a year and a half teaching fourth grade in order to get this opening—and now I am

"You'd better get up there in a hurry—they're tearing the room apart!"

confronted with a mob of hooligans and the messiest classroom in the building!"

I suppose it had not occurred to them that I had a grievance; they were so busy nursing theirs. Well, it had not occurred to me, either, until the Lord had reminded me. They began to slump in their seats, avoiding my eyes and casting furtive, ashamed glances at each other. The bold, defiant pose was quickly collapsing, replaced by a stunned confusion, which I thought I'd better take advantage of.

I confiscated the radio. I ordered the graffiti washed off the chalkboards and the desks, and the paper picked up from the floor. I dictated an impossible list of concrete goals which had to be achieved before they could graduate in June, a list that only an idealistic fourth grade teacher could have compiled, but it served its purpose. I had laid down a course, and I appeared to be a martinet who would keep them on it.

By the time they went home for lunch they had forgotten that I had been a primary teacher and were already complaining that I was tougher than the other two upper grade teachers combined.

We had a beautiful semester together. It would never have happened without the passwords provided by the Lord.

I talk a lot. In spates. Whenever I can find a sympathetic ear, my spouse says. Now, one would think that in sixty years of rapping, a person would have learned to handle the language to his or her advantage. Not necessarily so. Some people can create the best of impressions until they open their mouths and begin to speak. I am of that company. There are days when I should not be allowed out of the house, days when it is all I can do to get past the "How-do-you-dos" and the "Fine, thank-yous" without making a fool of myself by speaking the wrong word at the wrong time before a cloud of sharp-eared witnesses.

Maybe it's the reclusive life I have been living that has caused my social graces to atrophy; maybe it's the onset of old age that is responsible for my "tact erosion." It could even be that there is something of the fool about me, for didn't Solomon say in the tenth chapter of Ecclesiastes that "words from the mouth of a wise man are gracious, the lips of a fool consume him" (v. 12)?

I have said a great many regrettable and ridiculous things in my life. Mercifully, with the passage of time, I have been able to forget most of them. Only the most bizarre come back to haunt me now and then in the insomnious hours of the night. It is a chronic affliction, this misguided candor of mine, and I have told my husband that I am opting for cremation, simply because I cannot imagine being interred with both feet in my mouth—and that, I am certain, is how they are most likely to find me.

There *have* been occasions, especially during times of crisis—when I have had the good sense to pray *beforehand* and the wisdom to rely on the Lord *during*—that I managed to produce pearls instead of toads, profundities instead of inanities. It is a marvelous experience to find oneself in an impossible situation and then to be literally delivered by "words aptly spoken." By "apples of gold in settings of silver."

9
Hoist with Her Own Petard!

In the era just after the high school dress code had been declared unconstitutional, all the female students had taken to wearing skin-tight blue jeans and their brothers' or fathers' plaid flannel shirts, and they combed their long hair so that it continually flopped into their faces and had to be pushed back behind their ears every five seconds or so to let in a little light.

I should have known there was something wrong with Elfrieda the day she walked into my junior English class. Especially after I ascertained that she was a student, not a student-teacher.

Elfrieda wafted into my classroom on a cloud of Chantilly, fetchingly outfitted in a pastel pantsuit and a matching blouse that tied in a romantic bow under her chin. Her long blonde tresses were fashioned in such a style that both of her eyes were visible—and why not? They were immense, cornflower-blue, impacting eyes.

Elfrieda was such a refreshing sight—such a young lady amidst a generation of hooligans and hoydens—that I expected great things from her. I wasn't surprised when she approached me the first day to see if I would take her on as an aide. With a great deal of reluctance, I refused. "I never use aides," I told her. "I like to do my own correcting, to keep my fingers on the pupil's pulse, you know."

Undaunted, she was back at my desk the following day; pristine, dotted-Swiss blouse over a modified pink

Elfrieda wafted into my classroom on a cloud of Chantilly . . .
I expected great things from her.

crinoline, and ballet-type slippers, with narrow velvet ribbons restraining her flowing hair. How happy I was to have her for her junior year! *And she looks as though she will love Jane Austen and the Brontes,* I thought as she approached my desk.

This time she had come to ask if she could help me by recording my class grades—a time-consuming job involving five classes, daily quizzes, and weekly essays. What made it worse, I kept two separate records, one for myself and an official one which had to be turned in at semester's end. Again I refused, and again with a good deal of regret, explaining somewhat facetiously that recording grades was the only fun I got out of teaching anymore.

Elfrieda wore a royal blue pinwale corduroy jumper over a cornflower blue silk blouse on her third attempt to break down my resistance. Her hair was caught up in a chignon at the back of her head and the fluff of golden bangs over her wide eyes gave her an even more innocent appearance.

"How would you like me to clean out and organize your drawers and closets? I could make it a lot more efficient for you."

I recoiled in mock horror; telling her for what I hoped was the last time that I never used aides and that I had this thing about having to get away from it all in a deserted broom closet between classes. She laughed along with me, and I thought I had taken care of the matter once and for all. But a few days later, there she was again.

I don't remember what Elfrieda was wearing on this occasion, perhaps because what she said was so unnerving. Without preamble, she plunged right in: "Last year when I was in Mr. Short's English class I took attendance and sent out cut slips and everything. Mr. Short never had to worry about a thing."

Before I could do more than raise an eyebrow at the impropriety of that situation—attendance books are legal documents, and no one is supposed to touch them except the teacher in charge—she went on: "This year I'm Miss Bartlett's division secretary, and I handle all her attendance records for division and all the cut slips from her classes. You know there just isn't time during division period for a teacher to do all of that and take care of announcements and—"

She had not intended to raise my ire; in fact, she was surprised at my reaction and the lecture that followed. She left, not at all humbled but evidently convinced that we were not compatible; she never asked again if she could work for me.

Sometime around the fourth week of school, Elfrieda began to absent herself from my class two or three days a week. Routinely I checked the day's absence bulletin each time to see if she was listed as being absent from school. If not, I could assume she was cutting my class, and then I would send a cut slip to her division teacher.

Most of Elfrieda's absences from class appeared to be cuts, but the forms I sent to her division teacher came back to me with illegible scrawls that Elfrieda obligingly translated for me. Some, according to her, read "Sorry," meaning the teacher had erred in leaving Elfrieda's name off the bulletin. Some read "Excused," which Elfrieda informed me meant she had been there for division, but then had become ill and received permission to go home. I was not quite satisfied with the answers I was getting, but I still trusted the impeccable grooming, the innocent blue eyes, and the bold approach—unacquainted as I was with the criminal mind.

When I saw that Elfrieda was going to fail her first quarter, I decided that I would have to take some positive action myself, rather than turn the matter over to her division teacher, since the division teacher seemed to be turning all of her work over to Elfrieda.

"When's the best time to call your home, Elfrieda? I'd like to talk to your mother."

"My mother's a nurse, and she's on the three to midnight shift now. In a couple of weeks she'll be back on days."

"No problem. I'll call her during the school day."

"Oh, I don't think you'd better. She sleeps all day. Anyway, she keeps the phone turned down and probably wouldn't even hear it."

"When do you think she'll be back on days?"

"I'll let you know."

"Good, you do that. I hope it's soon. In the meantime, I'd appreciate your showing up for class every day!"

She did, for about two weeks. Then, evidently the strain became too much, and she began to cut again. Oh, she never admitted she was cutting. It was always her division teacher's mistake, or a clerical error, or an early dismissal. I could have handed the problem to her counselor, but I had a proprietary feeling about this case. I think I still cherished the hope that Elfrieda was innocent or at least the victim of circumstance.

Elfrieda stopped one day to tell me that her mother would be home that afternoon.

"Fine! Tell your mother I'll call about three thirty."

When I arrived home, I took only enough time to kick off my shoes and hug my dog before going to the phone. In my hand I had my grade and attendance books. I settled down for a long discussion and dialed the Jones' number.

"Hello! Is this Mrs. Jones, Elfrieda's mother?"

"Yes."

"Well, this is Mrs. Reichel, Elfrieda's English teacher. Did she tell you I would call?"

"Yes."

Oh, fine, I thought. *A compulsive non-talker!*

"Did she tell you what the problem is?"

"Yes."

I rolled my eyes at Everett who was sitting nearby, eavesdropping. "You *do* realize that she failed her first quarter? She *did* bring her coursebook home for you to sign?"

"Yes, she did."

"And you know that she's been cutting my class two and three times a week?"

"Yes."

"And that she's been forging her teachers' signatures in an effort to conceal her cuts?"

"Yes."

"Do you have any suggestions as to what we can do to help Elfrieda?"

98

"No, not really—"

I don't know how long this frustrating interview went on. I do know that I "lost my cool" and let my exasperation take over before I finally hung up. I sat there beside the phone for a few minutes thinking over the conversation that had taken place. Something didn't ring quite true. Parents become either angry or apologetic when confronted with their children's delinquency. Mrs. Jones had been completely unmoved. Then I began to wonder if maybe a hoax had been perpetrated. There was only one way to find out. I dialed the Jones' house again.

"Mrs. Jones? This is Mrs. Reichel again."

There was a long pause before the familiar "Yes."

"I've been thinking over the strange conversation you and I just had, and I am wondering if maybe someone is trying to play a trick on me. Your reactions to my complaints about Elfrieda are so untypical. Parents usually become angry with me, or their child, or the whole school system, and spend a half hour telling me about it—or they are shocked and apologetic and promise that they will take steps to see that their child will straighten out. You seemed so—so uncaring." I gave the voice at the other end a chance to contradict me, but there was no response.

"Mrs. Jones?"

"Yes?"

"You know, I really don't think this is Elfrieda's mother speaking. I think—"

She broke in before I could tell her just who I thought it was. In angry and highly indignant tones, loud and clear and defensive—and unwittingly self-incriminatory—she declared:

"THIS *IS* MY MOTHER SPEAKING!"

Well, I would like to leave the story at that point, but a reader might wonder what happened to Elfrieda. Her counselor suggested that she leave school. Not just because of the cutting incidents and the impersonations on the phone. There was the matter of the extra coursebook that she had stolen and which she filled in herself—

with straight A's, so that her parents were convinced she was a brilliant student. And there were the other truant classmates in her division who had depended on Elfrieda to cover for them in her job as division secretary.

There is an old Latin saying: *Fronti nulla fides* ("No reliance can be placed on appearance."), which, paraphrased, means "So much for innocent blue eyes!"

10
The Teacher Personality

After eighteen years of teaching, I am left with four London Fogs, six pairs of orthopedic oxfords, eight capacious handbags, and a firmly entrenched, fully developed Teacher Personality. The clothes and the handbags ought to last me to my grave. And so, says Everett, my long-suffering spouse, will my T.P.

Perhaps I'd better explain that before becoming a teacher I was a soft-spoken, easily intimidated, insecure, unopinionated, and submissive bore. A bachelor of education degree and a couple of years of classroom teaching changed all that. Oh, I am still a bore, but an officious and noisy one. Everett reminded me of that one Friday night in Chicago, a few years back, when I was still teaching.

We were having a snack at Lockwood Castle, having completed our weekly grocery shopping across the street at Dominick's. Occupying the booth next to ours were two intensely voluble women, whose voices were the penetrating, projecting kind that discourages all other conversation in the vicinity. Since there was no other table or booth available, and because at first their dialogue seemed a lot more animated and enthusiastic than any my husband and I could work up, we resigned ourselves to listening while we dealt with our club sandwiches and chocolate sodas.

We learned early on that we were tuned in to a couple of schoolteachers out on the town. From their onion soup to their Swiss steak to their last spoonfuls of hot fudge sundae, they "talked shop"—with relish. Their conversation was laced with educationese like "reading readiness," "overcompensation," "brain dysfunction," and so on. The faded blonde in the purple blouse spoke of how she coped with Larry's lack of coordination, and the redhead in the green plaid interrupted with Melissa's mirror vision and her successes in handling it. Then the blonde cut her short with a recital of how she had been able to turn Jimmy's nonverbal skills into a productive exercise; but she was soon silenced by the redhead's account of how she had harnessed hyperactive Pauline.

"It's so sad," I clucked to Everett as we walked out of the restaurant.

"What is?"

"Those two women. They were so intense; taking themselves so seriously."

"What's wrong with that?"

"It's Friday night! They should leave all that behind them. They hadn't even relaxed yet; their motors were still racing. I'll bet they didn't taste anything they ate; they were so preoccupied with school affairs!"

Everett unlocked my side of the car and held the door open. Before closing it he said rather cautiously, "You didn't notice any resemblance between those two in there and anybody you know?"

By the time he had slipped into his seat and had the key in the ignition, I caught on. "*I* don't go on like that!" I protested.

He didn't argue. He recognizes the eloquence of silence.

We pulled out from the curb and drove a few blocks south on Central before we were halted by lowering crossing gates at the railroad crossing.

"Do I?" I resumed.

"Do you *what?*" he asked, already having forgotten the question.

"Do I go on like those women; yakking away after school, *about* school?"

"Well, no. Only when you meet other teachers. And you sure go out of your way to meet other teachers!"

I knew well what Everett was referring to. Since I had begun teaching, our social life had been radically altered. I turned down most invitations, too tired to socialize. When I did accept, I didn't enjoy myself unless I found another teacher with whom I could talk. Fortunately, I could sniff out another pedagogue at twenty paces. The attraction was generally mutual, and while the rest of the assemblage discussed P.T. or E.T. or fishing on their coming trip to Tasmania, my confrere and I drew strength from one another's academic anecdotes.

"How do you find each other?" Everett wanted to know. "I could set you down in the middle of a AARP convention and within fifteen minutes you would have your own cozy caucus of fifteen or twenty retired schoolteachers!"

I don't know how we do it or why. Call it self-defense or the will to survive. I do know that on occasions when I have been the only teacher on the premises I have been backed into corners by irate parents who have a bone to pick. It made no difference that I taught in a district far removed from theirs. It's always open season on teachers.

"Another strike?" they demanded. "What are you after this time?"

"Another raise?" they sneered. "For only nine months' work? And all those school holidays! Everybody should have it so good!"

"What about those reading scores?" they argued. "When are you teachers going to begin teaching the kids to read?"

Nor did I have to go to a party to get shot at. When I stood on a corner waiting for a bus, attaché case in hand and shoulders slumped in fatigue, I became an invitation to total strangers to accost me, as one woman did.

"You're a teacher, aintcha? I knew it was either that or a cemetery lot saleslady, what with the briefcase. Say, what's wrong with the schools today? They ain't teachin' the kids nothin' nowadays. It ain't like when I was in school."

In the beauty parlor I was a sitting duck. Most of the

hairdressers in my day had spoiled, overindulged boys, who kept interrupting my gilding by trotting in and whining, "Ma, I can't find the ice cream bars [or the popsicles, or the Twinkies, or whatever]!" And as soon as they disappeared to stoke their furnaces, I was regaled and grilled in turn regarding the injustices and biases on the part of principals, teachers, and counselors who just didn't understand Junior. If I spoke candidly, there was the real possibility I might end up with a limp wave. If I restrained myself, I would be given a good tight perm atop an excruciating migraine.

I switched meat markets because after my butcher discovered I was a teacher he stopped calling me "Dearie" and "Honey," the usual forms of familiar address in that kind of establishment, and instead used me as a sounding board for all his frustrations concerning the teenagers of that era.

"The schools have been too permissive," he ranted, pointing an accusing finger at me. "That's what it is, all right—the schools!"

When I was summoned for jury duty, I anticipated a ten-day hiatus, so I brought along Ann Morrow Lindbergh's *Bring Me a Unicorn* to read while sitting in the waiting room. Instead, I was locked in with eleven of my peers, who took every opportunity to remind me that schools and teachers were not doing their job. "Oh, not you, of course," they would rush to add. "It's all the young ones—" Or, "It's all those old, doddering spinsters who don't understand the young people—" And the foreman of our jury loved to quote the old Shavian maxim—he quoted it and taught it to all the rest of the jurors, so they could take it home with them—"Those who can, do. Those who can't, teach."

I suppose it was the constant intimidation that made us teachers seek the company of fellow sufferers and actually contributed to the development of our teacher personalities. Who would deny the truism that the oppressed ultimately become the oppressors?

There was another element at work on us teachers—besides intimidation—that transformed a good many of us into stereotypical old ladies, meddlesome and officious. Power corrupts, they say, and having under one's daily supervision some two hundred students, most of whom march to one's cadence, is a heady business. If one has an ounce of authoritarianism lurking within his soul, a few years of teaching will cause it to burgeon into the most awesome imperiousness. At least, that was my experience. Regrettably, this new personality was not something I could shuck the minute I stepped out of the classroom. I took it home with me, out with me, and even into my retirement.

My Teacher Personality has turned me into one of those obnoxious persons who have to be in charge or else they panic—in an airplane, a speedboat, or the passenger seat of almost anything. Even in churches or concert halls I now tend to sit in the back, so that the whole scene is under my surveillance. I wasn't this way before I became a teacher, only after—*well* after.

I have become dauntless and tactless; I speak out whenever I think the occasion demands it. It didn't matter to me that I was a stranger in a Presbyterian church in downstate Illinois; I still turned around and shushed the pair of biddies who were gossiping a mile a minute during the organ prelude. Everett was embarrassed by my boldness, but then he doesn't have the same appreciation for organ music that I do.

On a vacation trip to the West Coast, I imperiled my husband and two daughters by my inability to mind my own business. We had stopped at a campground in Oregon. Because it was a hot and dusty day, we unhitched our camper and drove down to the camp swimming hole—a beautiful spot, no more than a bend in the river, but shaded and cool.

Several families were trying to enjoy the facility but were prevented from doing so by a gang of motorcyclists who were drinking and cursing and riding wildly all over the embankments, narrowly missing the waders. A frail, slightly built fellow in his sixties had taken on one of the gang members who had dismounted from his bike, but he was getting nowhere. In fact, the leather-clad hoodlum had already assumed that ludicrous but threatening stance, toe-to-toe, expanded chest, that I

105

recognized so well from the elementary school playgound. He was about to flatten Mr. Good Citizen.

The teacher in me responded. I jumped out of our car before Everett could grab me and elbowed my way indignantly between the two men, wagging my index finger under the nose of the bearded cyclist.

"Aren't you ashamed of yourself?" I demanded. "Why don't you go find someone your own age and size to pick on?"

I continued with more detention hall diction, following him with my authoritative digit as he backed away from me and towards the safety of his bike. Before I let him get away, I promised him and the rest of his cohorts who had gathered around out of curiosity: "What's more, we're going right down to the camp office to call the police!"

They fled, every one of them, on their Harley-Davidsons. I was triumphant, but on the point of collapse. *Oh, Samson! The jawbone of a teacher can also accomplish much!*

Not all confrontations end in glory, however. I had an errand in the Loop after school, so instead of walking home I boarded the east-bound Addison bus. Well, it really wasn't a matter of boarding; I merely stopped struggling and let myself be carried on the tidal wave of a hundred or more students, only a few of whom knew me well enough to avoid trampling me to death.

Once the doors were closed and the bulging bus on its way, I noticed a most annoying odor—that of cigarettes being lit up. It was after three o'clock; I had already signed out, and my working day was over. No matter, my teacher reflexes were still in operation. "Search and destroy" was the signal I was getting. I left my snug perch at the front of the bus and wormed my way slowly toward the rear, following my nose, finally sighting the culprits, three girls and a boy, puffing away hungrily.

I could have stopped there; they had not spotted me through their self-created smoke screen; they were off school property—this was really a problem for the CTA to handle—but the teacher in me refused to back down.

"Aren't you ashamed of yourself? Why don't you find some-one your own age and size to pick on?"

"Let me see your I.D.'s!" I ordered the malefactors. They looked at me, stunned by the five-foot-three, disheveled grandmother standing over them.

"Who are *you?*" one of them challenged. An innocent bystander introduced me.

"That's Mrs. Reichel, my English teacher."

"Yeah, she's a teacher, Mike," someone else corroborated in a taunting voice. "Better do what she tells you!"

Well, they did what I told them—handed over their I.D.'s and extinguished their cigarettes. By the time our business was concluded, I was only a minute away from my transfer point, so I hurried back through the crowd to the rear exit. Did I mention that it was a spring day and the bus windows were open? Well, it was, and they were, and the raucous farewell I received as the bus slowly pulled away from the curb on which I was standing undid me to the point that, even though I completed my trip downtown by subway train, when I arrived there I wandered aimlessly through the stores in a state of genuine trauma, my mission forgotten.

"I hope you learned your lesson," Everett said, massaging my aching feet and drying my tears.

"I have," I admitted. "From now on I'll stay away from buses; I'll take a cab instead."

I did, too, for about a year, and then on a Sunday afternoon I boarded the Milwaukee Avenue bus at the Jefferson Park terminal on the last leg of a 280-mile trip from Door County. I had survived the drive to the Sturgeon Bay airport, the twin-engine Beechcraft to O'Hare, the airport bus to Jefferson Park—no reason why I couldn't manage the fifteen minute bus ride home.

At the terminal I settled myself in the rear of the bus, anticipating the crowd of Sunday shoppers who would be boarding at Irving Park. Also, when it came time for me to disembark, I would be only a step away from the rear door. Two teenagers also got on at the terminal. Instead of sitting, they positioned themselves at the rear exit, successfully blocking that door and forcing those who wanted to leave the bus to do so by the front door.

Some of the disgruntled passengers complained to the bus driver as they got off. He responded with a helpless shrug. My anger mounted as I neared my destination. A few months before, I would have told myself, "Forget it; it's not worth a scene!" Now I felt I had a charge to keep on behalf of all those frightened citizens who had caved in and exited at the front of the bus and all those who had yet to leave.

I rose well in advance of my stop, train case in one hand, purse/portmanteau in the other, and I confronted the teenagers.

"Move it!" I snapped. A deplorable expression, I'll admit, but it has a great deal of shock value coming from the lips of a graying grandmother.

Their mouths dropped open; their eyes widened, but they didn't budge. One of them recovered enough to protest, "You got plenty a room, lady!", referring to the six inches between himself and his friend.

I ignored him, continued to glare, and then repeated, this time considerably louder, "You heard me! Move it!"

That did it. They stepped aside. Oh, not with any alacrity, but they gave me plenty of room. I pulled the cord, and the bus ground to a halt. I descended to the curb, my knees turned to water, but my confidence fully restored.

I suppose that's why I agreed a few weeks later when a lovely lady called to ask me if I would appear on a radio talk show. Not as an author, but as a teacher who happened to have written a book. I was undaunted by the title of the show, "Meet the Experts." If I didn't know all the answers after seventeen years of teaching, then who did? Besides, hadn't I been guest speaker and panel member at several PTA sessions and performed admirably, or at least been told so? I was confident I could field any questions thrown at me, especially since my gracious hostess promised she would explain to the audience that my expertise lay in the teaching of English at the secondary level, and that I would appreciate questions relative to that area.

I was prepared to answer arguments about censorship of books, student apathy, and Christian schools versus public schools. However, the callers had other ideas; they wanted to know what I thought about the independent study programs, open classrooms, PACE, Dick and Jane versus McGuffey, and so on.

"You *could* have said, 'I don't know.' Or, 'That's not my field.'" Everett suggested, an hour after the program was part of history, while I cried into my Coke. He was too nice to say, "You didn't have to show your ignorance by pretending to have all the answers!"

Because teachers are always in the limelight in the classroom, many of us tend to upstage no matter where we find ourselves. Since we are the final word before our trusting pupils, we are inclined to consider ourselves the repository of all knowledge. In social situations outside the classroom we interrupt; we dogmatize; we overbear. The onus of leadership weighs heavily upon our shoulders. If *we* don't know the answers, who does? Poets, they say, suffer from the same delusion.

Everett is convinced that some day he and I will be passengers on a 767 heading for Seattle when a wild-eyed, bushy-haired character will leap to his feet, a grenade in each hand, demanding the plane change its course, and my Teacher Personality will respond; I will rush up to this maniac, wagging my finger, and say, "Tch, tch, you ought to be ashamed of yourself! Give me those this instant, and go right back to your seat, or I will send you down to the disciplinarian!"

I promise Everett that I will reform. Myself, that is. Not the world around me. But then we get into a restaurant line, and a cigar smoker lights up in front of me. My resolve *dissolves*, and I remount my white charger.

"My good man," I begin in tutorial tones as Everett looks off into space, disassociating himself from the scene. "I have sensitive sinuses—"

11
I Seen a Million Sparrows

Given the authority, I would close the Chicago schools in the middle of May, for it is then that the wheels of learning begin to decelerate–give or take a few days–depending on the humidity of the Chicago weather and the performance of the Chicago Cubs. Any learning that takes place after spring vacation in April is accidental–pupil resistance is at its highest then, and teacher energy is on the wane.

Especially mine. It is only the lure of the paycheck and the voice of my conscience that prevent me from running away with the circus. As it is, I stay by the stuff with reluctance and contribute to the delinquency of spring by raising the windows high and letting in the music of the ice cream trucks and drag racers and the smells of lilac blossoms and burning rubber. I decorate the walls with new posters splashed with radicalisms from Thoreau and Emerson. I join the conspiracy of spring. My priorities become pied. My lesson plans deteriorate.

No harm done, as far as the honors classes are concerned. They don't mind my call to abandon participles and gerunds for a day to splash around in e.e. cummings's "just spring," "mudluscious," and "puddle wonderful." No twisting of the arm is necessary. They'll gladly drop their grammar texts to take a walk beside a stone wall in Vermont with Robert Frost, and they need no second invitation to taste to intoxication "from tan-

111

kards in pearl" with Emily Dickinson. But those are the gifted students, the aware ones. I can let them run free one day and whistle them back the next.

That is not true of the pupils in my Essentials class, and it is especially not true of Juan Esperanza Gonzalez, whose roots are in the San Juan barrio, whose T-shirts are emblazoned with slogans like Puerto Rican Power, and who sashays to the rum-tum-tumming of a very different and far-away drummer.

Juan's face is long and narrow and topped with a resplendent Afro coiffure. Barely sixteen years old, he nevertheless has managed to cultivate a wisp of a moustache and a sparse goatee. Because of his height, just over six feet, he has already been drafted by the basketball coach. That means he will resist the sophomore temptation to drop out of school and will probably remain with us for two—maybe three—more years. That is not to suggest he will increase substantially in knowledge during this time. The coach and the administration will settle happily for an increase in his stature.

Juan is in my Essentials class because his reading level is considerably lower than his grade level. The average reading comprehension score for any given Essentials class is about fourth grade. The level of sophistication, on the other hand, is extremely high, since most, not all, of the Essentials kids have come up by way of the streets.

Truancy is endemic among this group, especially in the spring, so I tighten the reins. No flights of fancy or flirting with frivolity. I do not deviate from the routine established and followed since the beginning of the year. The regimen is simple: spelling and vocabulary on Monday, the *Reader's Digest* and related lessons Tuesday through Thursday, spelling test and oral review on Friday, and a simple novel each quarter. It is a comfortable pattern for them, and they resent any deviation. It is Dullsville for me, but if I have learned anything in my eighteen years of teaching, it is to stay with what "works."

I had to remind myself of that one warm Monday in May as I was making a few notes in my lesson plan

112

book—there is a security in sameness. The following day would be a *Digest* day. I was not looking forward to the assignment, for we had already exhausted all the high-interest stories in the current magazine. There was one story left, an essay on English sparrows. How to make that article as gripping as an Alpine landslide or a hijacking over the Pacific was a problem I was going to have to resolve.

In the meantime I kept one eye on the class, all bent industriously over spelling papers and dictionaries. All, that is, except Juan Gonzalez, who gazed peacefully into space and thought his own thoughts. Juan lived in a land of eternal spring. His body had to obey the dictates of compulsory education, but his mind roamed free. He was on my class roster and had an assigned seat in my classroom, but he was never really *of* the group, merely *in* it. Instructions given to the class in general did not reach Juan until twenty minutes later, unless I had time to deliver them personally and emphatically. Even then, he was seldom able to persevere until the end, so tenuous was his hold on reality.

Let me give you an example or two. In the middle of a discussion of the energy crisis and how it might affect the students' driving habits in the next twenty years, Juan, who cared nothing for relevancy, blurted out, "Hey, man, who knows where I kin get my lunch tickets?"

When seatwork was assigned, Juan would usually go through the motions of getting out his book, borrowing pen and paper, and then, realizing he didn't know where to go from there—even with the instructions a foot high on the chalkboard—would demand loudly, "Hey, man, what's goin' on here?"

"Oh, Juan, you are always out of step!" I despaired in one of our many conferences. Late, chronically late to class—and slow, irkingly slow to comprehend why he came at all. He smiles at my gentle chiding. It is impossible to be anything but gentle with him. I have tried indignation, but he responds with a helpless shrug of his shoulders. He apologizes sweetly, knowing an apology is

Juan lived in a land of eternal spring.

in order, but not knowing why. His eyes never lose the opaqueness that shuts me out.

If ever I felt I was "wasting my sweetness on the desert air," it was with Juan. *He is one of the unteachables*, I decided after months of prayer and endeavor. I had found no way to communicate with him. He was totally out of sync with the academic scene.

On Tuesday I go ahead with my lesson on sparrows. To motivate the young people, I narrate several anecdotes about our family's experiences with birds. I make rough sketches at the chalkboard of the smallest visitor to our country feeders, a hummingbird hooked on sugarwater tinted red; and the largest guest, a neighbor's malemute, who comes to forage after suet scraps dropped by the woodpeckers. I confess to the class my lack of enthusiasm for sparrows; admit that with the exception of the melodious white-throated variety, I would just as soon those drab, dull birds frequent another cafeteria than ours.

"But," I hasten to add, flourishing my magazine, "we've got an author here who finds sparrows *interesting!* Can you imagine? Interesting enough to write about." I pull out the scorn and skepticism stops—hamming it up is part of teaching. "And not only that—here's a magazine that paid him somewhere in the neighborhood of a thousand dollars for his story! Let's find out why!" If nothing else piques their interest, the thousand dollars does.

And then for thirty minutes we read and talk about the constancy, the cleverness, the family devotion of sparrows. We learn about the precarious lives they lead, stalked by cats, owls, and automobiles. We heed the author's reminder that sparrows are a "link with that great, free, natural world outside a metropolis." He tells us that there is no other wild creature that does so much to cheer us up, and that out of the whole world we are the ones he has chosen for his friends.

The bell calls a halt. *Ho-hum and thank goodness*, I think, and race the kids to the door. *It's the last class of the day, spring is popping out all over, and if I hurry home I might catch the final innings of the Cubs versus St. Louis contest.*

Then Wednesday—another one to scratch off the calendar. Twenty-seven days to go—will I survive them? Sparrows are past history as I take the attendance. Only six students absent—make that five—Juan will be here in his own good time.

"Turn to page two-oh-three in your *Digest*. The article on 'Monte Alban, the City of the Gods.' " I distribute mimeographed sheets for a word search and start the students off in the right direction. Quiet settles over the room, and I sit at my desk to catch whatever breeze may pass between the open windows and the door. I forget Juan. I generally do, even though his tardiness is a fixed habit that no number of detentions has been able to cure; even though his entrances are breathless and, until I threaten him with removal from the basketball team, noisily dramatic.

I wool-gather, lulled into a mesmeric euphoria by the combination of weather and spring weariness and the sweet sound of pen on paper. It has been an interminably long day, and I am bone-tired and on the edge of nodding.

The sound of running feet in the hall brings me back quickly. It has to be Juan. I change the absent slash after his name to a "T" for tardy and look up as he appears in the doorway. I am ready for him with a worksheet, pen, and paper—my finger on my lips to remind him of his manners. But this is to be a day unlike any other.

Juan excitedly brushes aside the papers I offer him. He ignores my cue to be quiet. He seems oblivious to his classmates, who, sensing his agitation, stop working to watch. I rise from my chair, alarmed by the beatific, transported expression on Juan's face. The veil is gone; we are making eye contact.

"Hey, man!" he shouts, and I put my hand on his arm to lead him out into the hall. He shrugs off the restraint.

"Hey, man! Missus Reichels, you gotta listen! You know dem little birds you wuz talkin' 'bout yestaday?

Dem sparrows? Man! I seen a million of 'em on my way to school dis mornin'!"

There is disagreement among teachers as to which is the most grueling time of the year. Some say it is the settling-in period in September, when the paperwork mounts and the continual revision of classes frustrates any attempt at systematic teaching. Others maintain it is the final quarter, when the heat and exhaustion take their toll.

I hold with the latter. "Whan that Aprille with his shoures soote/The droghtes of March hath perced to the roote,"* then I begin to come unglued. My husband stops asking when he picks me up after work, "Did you have a good day?" Even Poquito, our Chihuahua, keeps a respectful distance until I have had an hour or two to unwind. Spring is the season when I vow daily to leave the classroom and never return; when I try to convince myself that my husband and I can survive on his meager pension; when in my insomnia I draft letter after letter of resignation.

And then there's a dramatic breakthrough—the scales fall from a student's eyes, and a Juan Gonzalez sees a million sparrows where yesterday there were none; or a shy Linda Witkowski, unsure of herself in honors class, discovers all alone and before anyone else can hazard a guess what Poe is saying in his poem "Israfel."

That is all I ask for. That is all I need. I have strength for another few days.

* Geoffrey Chaucer, *The Canterbury Tales.*

Moody Press, a ministry of the Moody Bible Institute, is designed for education, evangelization, and edification. If we may assist you in knowing more about Christ and the Christian life, please write us without obligation: Moody Press, c/o MLM, Chicago, Illinois 60610.